You Can Be a Software Architect

SASI Publishing

www.sasicentral.com

Product of the United States of America

Publisher's Cataloging-in-Publication data
Correa, Bett.
A title of the book : You Can Be a Software Architect.
ISBN-13: 978-1481865630

1. The main category of the book —Software — Software Architecture— Software Engineering

First Edition

Troy,
May all your dreams come true!

Bett Correa
08-02-2013

Table of Contents

How to read this book

This book has five parts:

First, Part 1: ***What Is a Software Architect?*** describes what an architect does for a living, and why it's important. You should read this section to get on the same page with our vocabulary.

Second, Part 2: ***How did I become a Software Architect?*** describes my biographical information. You can skip this part if you want to get right to the meat of the book. It's not required. I describe the startup companies I worked at, and the lessons I learned at each.

Third, Part 3: ***Steps to Become a Software Architect*** describes in detail the steps that you can follow to become a software architect in a small to large enterprise.

Fourth, Part 4: ***Best Practices for Effective Software Architecture*** describes the set of best practices that all architects need to follow to be effective.

Fifth, Part 5: ***The Future*** describes the future of software architecture and the next steps on your personal journey. I recommend you read it straight from beginning to end and then reference the Best Practices when needed. It's important to read Part 1 to ensure you understand the type of software architecture covered in this book.

Part 1: What is a Software Architect?
Why Architecture is Important

Developing software is one of the most exciting, challenging undertakings a human can endeavor. All software has architecture. The question is whether the software's architecture is intentional or desultory? This chapter is about why intentional architecture is important.

In his book, *Good to Great*, Jim Collins says that there are three steps to having a great company: Disciplined people, disciplined thought, and disciplined action. Architects are disciplined people who rigorously go through software's requirements and find a design that will meet those requirements. Architecture is produced by this disciplined thought and leads to disciplined action in implementation.

A lack of solid architecture can cause your company huge embarrassment. Just looking at the news while I am writing this shows me two huge examples of where computer architecture damaged the company. The recent break into Epsilon shows that architecture is crucial for keeping your company's reputation. Southwest Airlines' computer system crashed and caused the grounding of all their flights.

There's no evidence that systems are getting simpler, rather even as architects strive for more streamlined systems, end users demands more and more functionality. As software becomes easier to use, its design becomes more complex. Mobility, security, larger and larger data sets, intuitive interfaces, shorter and shorter response times all require not only intentional, but advanced designs. Architects are and will become more and more crucial for the success of a business.

Figure 1: Imagine a Building Built without an Architect

Software systems can be the most important asset a company owns. It can give them an edge over their competitors. Software systems often are the center of the company's core competency. And yet many times companies consider the architecture of their software as an afterthought.

Imagine a hotel company slapping together concrete, wood, nails, and paint to create a hotel without commissioning an architect to design it first. A hotel can cost 20 to 70 million dollars. I've personally worked on a software project that cost 60 million. Software is key and expensive, it must be designed with the same care that a building is designed.

The importance of architecture is almost so fundamental it's difficult to explain. There're a few levels when looking at architecture. First level is just documenting the architecture. Companies usually have several modules in their software, if not several systems, each with a variety of modules. Those modules often are distributed and client server. At first the architecture might live in the minds of the developers, but as folks come and go, soon an architecture needs to at least be documented. This documented architecture allows new developers to get the concept of the architecture quickly. At some point, the system won't be meeting the needs of the business anymore. On that day, you'll need to create an intentional architecture. You might need to use the existing architecture documentation to create the *To Be* architecture.

Second level is creating a *To Be* architecture before you even start. This is a rare case. If you get to do this, consider yourself lucky. Usually you have existing systems that need to be patched to create some new functionality. Creating architecture from scratch means that you will need to have the business thoroughly document their requirements. The architect should be heavily involved in the gathering of the documentation to ensure they completely understand what is needed and why.

Often the "why" will lead to efficiencies in the design. Business folks are notorious for not knowing what they want, but they do know <u>why</u> they want it. As will be discussed later, the architect must really get into the heads of the business people, and deliver what they really need.

The more complex the system, the more important it is to have an architecture that is well thought through. There are lots of tools to use to ensure your consideration of all the salient features of your software before you start writing the code. There are lots of methods of developing the software.

The architecture of software can even allow a company to branch into different markets. For example, assume a software company has a core competency in creating book layout software for standard book publishers. Their architecture is based on an infrastructure that has plug-in modules. Each module has a specific function. After finding their software is very popular with the standard book publishing companies, they realize that they can leverage the infrastructure and build some modules specifically for the needs of online book publishing companies. Now the company is twice as profitable due to excellent software architecture.

A company that employs an excellent software architect can rest assured that their software should meet the business's requirements. Of course software architects can't make contingency plans for every possible thing that could go wrong, but careful thoughtful design can identify the probable flaws.

When you consider how important software is to a business's core competency and reputation, you realize that the software architecture is one of the most important decisions a business can make. Thus the software architect is one of the most important people in the company. This is why you want to be a software architect.

The architect is one of the most important people in the entire company because they hold the keys to the company's software, which is central to the company's core competency and reputation.

In order to create an architecture that meets all the requirements and supports the business function, the architect must take into account much that a developer doesn't need to worry about. The salient items that will impact the project need to be assessed.

When a developer is creating a function, they need to consider the requirements, the language, and the hardware limitations. But an architect has a wider scope of things that they must navigate.

Architects have the hardest job in the company. The architect must learn quickly.

They must know all things:

- The Direction the Company is Going In
- The Current Systems Requirements
- The *To Be* Systems Requirements
- Politics
- The Budget
- The Timelines

Let's go thru these salient items one by one.

The Direction the Company is Going in

If your company is moving towards client server technology, then you shouldn't recommend an architecture that uses mainframes.

Another direction is towards in-house development or off-the-shelf. This is often a very controversial subject in companies. The directions your company is going in will radically change your approach to the solution. You must find out what's the direction that the leaders are leaning. Often you'll be able to help make that decision on which way the company should go.

The Current Systems Requirements

Very rarely will you be able to start with a green field or a totally new system. Usually you have some existing infrastructure you need to work around.

All of these things are moving targets. Being able to keep up is always a challenge. The architect must be able to keep their finger on the pulse of the company, and to adapt to the changing environment.

No architect works alone, but instead is in constant communication with their business partners and IT partners. The architect acts as a channel between the business and the developers. Keeping track of what's going on in an unstructured environment is a key skill the architect possesses. The architect must be able to communicate well, and to keep on top of what is important.

Stakeholders in a project are those who have a vested interest in the outcome of the project. They are users, clients, customers, impacted system leads and developers. They attend many meetings with the clients to understand the requirements. They must make sure all the stakeholders give their input so they don't miss any salient data points. They must win the trust of those stakeholders in the project, so that those stakeholders will listen to them when they recommend an architecture solution.

The architect must know all these things, and then they must produce artifacts that document and communicates a system that meets the requirements.

Things are constantly changing, and the architect must quickly adjust to the changes. Every system will have different requirements and ways to be documented; thus the architect must be versatile and move accordingly.

Stakeholders

It's all about the people. As an architect you'll be faced with a large number of people who all have strong opinions about the project. This chapter will review some of the folks you must deal effectively with in order to be successful.

1. Clients
2. Users
3. Development Leadership
4. Project Managers
5. Developers
6. Testers
7. Trainers
8. The Public

Clients

Clients pay. That's the definition. Whoever is requesting the system change and paying for the change is the client. This group may be product development or some internal group. At the end of the day, they will determine if you successfully implemented their request. Get to know the drivers responsible for their requests. Understand their world view. What's their pain, and why. This knowledge will allow you to create a better design.

Users

Users will use your system. They can be the champion of you system or they can reject your system. Many systems fail to be used, and are discarded due to users unhappy with the end system. Depending on the politics of your org, your users may have more or less power, but regardless, the users can either buy in or reject. So make them your partners.

This is difficult because users live in a focused world. They want to get their job done. They learn tricks to do it. Users are very resourceful. I've seen them use all kinds of hacks and workarounds to make things happen. Imagine you are used to MS Word, and then MS releases a new version that is radically different. Now instead of just typing up your report, you need to relearn all the menus to get to be productive. This is the same way that users feel when you're publishing changes. But at the same time, as an architect you have a vision for the future, and your vision has new features. You have to balance adding new exciting features with keeping the users productive. Training is always a big ordeal for users and expensive to the business. To ensure that they are champions of your creation, involve them in the requirements documentation step. Review your design with them. The more they feel their input is being valued, the more they'll accept your system.

Development Leadership

Programmers who become managers are a special breed of people. You may want to take this track instead of architecture if you want to spend a lot time motivating folks to show up to work everyday instead of designing systems. The architect needs to have a very friendly relationship with all the development leadership. What you will find is that your architecture is a suggestion to the developers. Only the programmer's management can really "make them" code to your specifications, or for that matter show up to your meetings and participate. You can get the loyalty of the leadership by talking to them. Find out what's their pain, their motivations, their strategic direction. Find out what's important to them. Then make sure you consider those points in your design. Make sure they are involved in important decisions. In the end their resources need to code your design. Make sure they agree with your approach.

Project Managers

I am often asked, "What's the difference between architects and project managers?"

The main difference is that project managers are concerned with the timelines, running status meetings, defining tasks, assigning tasks to correct people, and following up with them to ensure the project is delivered on time.

Software architects are concerned with the technical design of the system. They will definitely run design meetings, give people action items, and follow up with them. But their purpose is to create and document the design of the system.

You and the project manager are going to be partners. You need to understand their desires, and work with them to do what you can to help the project deliver successfully. In big projects there will be dependencies between modules and systems. Your project manager will need you to help them understand those dependencies so that he or she can create the project plan correctly. You might also need to help price out the system to allow your project manager to provide system cost data to the clients.

Developers

Be very attentive to your developers. They need to both understand and give you feedback on your design. Sometimes developers are quiet, so you will have to prod them. Go sit with them and understand what they are thinking. Ask open questions and listen carefully. Often you'll learn important information that will impact your project and design. Don't waste their time on too many meetings. Make sure you create a clear agenda for every meeting you need them to attend. Make sure that they clearly understand any action items and due dates for each before the end of your meeting. If developers know you're not going to waste their time, they will willingly come to your design meetings.

Testers

Testers get overlooked, maligned and ignored by everyone in the SDLC. But, testers must fully understand your design if you want your project to be successful. Testers tend to be very methodical folks, and this can sometimes frustrate the more abstract architect, but this is their skill set. Make sure your documentation is easily grasped by your testers. Listen to their questions and concerns. The questions that testers ask often unveil gaps in your design. Even though this is painful, it's better to fill in the gaps in your design before the developers code the system.

Trainers

Users need to be trained on your new system or changes to an existing system. Trainers are responsible to ensure the users know how to use the system. The more the trainers understand how your system works the more effective they'll be in their job. Remember that if users reject your system, it doesn't matter how cool or efficient your system is, you will have failed.

The Public

Your system may impact the public. Make sure it's an ethical system. Do no harm at the very least. If it's a life support system, make sure that it's not going to fail!

Part 2: How did I become a Software Architect?
Community College Experience/Volunteer Work

Growing up in Key West doesn't a computer programmer usually make. The aqua green water, warm sea breeze, lush palm trees don't usually make a good breeding place for a geek, and yet that's where I grew up from the time I was 7 onwards. My family got our first computer in 1989 when my dad received money from the insurance company, due to a car accident. Instead of fixing the dent in our white VW bus, he bought an x86 Dos computer. I played Ant Run, Commander Keen, and Duke Nukem. I loved the computer from the beginning.

My future husband Tony's bright green eyes sparkled when he told me he'd written a program in his college class. It was 1995. I was only 16 at the time, and the world of programming was a mystery to me, so I sat next him on our family's x86 Windows 95 PC. He started up a Dos prompt and typed in *run names.exe*. A prompt came up and asked him for a name. He typed in "Bett" and hit enter. My very own name began filling the screen in all kinds of colors. I completely fell in love... with programming.

I started going to Florida Keys Community College the summer of 1996. I took Lotus 123. In the fall I took four classes including "Introduction to Computer Science." I fell deeper in love. I never doubted that I wanted to be a programmer. I watched "Hackers" and knew that I was on the right path. I took "C Programming," and reveled in the pointers and linked lists.

Sammer Hijazi, a Syrian with sparkling black eyes and a thick crew cut, taught my computer classes, and I'd ask him all kinds of questions. He challenged me constantly and pushed me hard to expand my mind. I took BASIC, COBOL, Intermediate C Programming, Advanced Topics in C Programming, and Visual Basic before I graduated with an Associate Degree in Science in Computer Programming and Applications.

While I was going to school, I worked in the graphics lab, which allowed me to become very good at Photoshop. I began to teach myself web development. I viewed the source of WebPages I liked. I copied them and began tweaking and playing. I was learning the hard way— by trial and error. Years later I took an html test, and the scorer said I had the highest score she'd ever seen. I never meant to memorize html. I just wrote so much code, that I got good at it. I put up a web page at "Geo Cities" just like everyone else. I wrote my own rollovers in JavaScript. Geez, that was freaking hard! I had a few different designs for Bettworld.com, my personal web site.

Around this time, I got a job as a weather observer at Key West International Airport. I worked the midnight shift there in the air traffic control tower. Working at night was perfect because I got to code all night and go to college during the day.

In 1999 my life changed forever when I watched "The Matrix." By then I was married, and Tony and I were huge sci-fi fans.

I immediately created a Matrix fan page. I modified Matrix pictures in Photoshop and got lots of hits. My page was number one in the search engine in 1999. I received at least one fan email every day. I always thought it was funny because everyone thought I was a dude. I spent most of my time on AOL back then. It was the main ISP (Internet Service Provider.) I had lots of friends whom I never met in 3D. But then I discovered something really special: IRC (Internet Relay Chat.) I joined an IRC chat for the Matrix and also found a graphics group. My new friends in IRC were awesome. The main leader in graphics was Razor. He asked me to write a webpage for the monthly graphics contest. I jumped at the chance to code. I wrote the script in CGI, (Common Gateway Interface) and in PERL. It was an amazing learning experience.

At this time I became good friends with a lady in my C class. She was a genius, and she introduced me to her genius husband. They ran an ISP. Her husband started showing me Linux. They let me help them crimp CAT 5 cables. I'd spend hours learning about how web servers worked with them. They were truly geeks, and I learned a lot about servers, routers and how the Internet worked.

This inspired me to build my own Linux box in 1999. So I gathered up some hardware from our small apartment and built the computer. Then I installed Red Hat. I compiled my kernel with a mouse driver for a 3 button mouse. Fancy! I connected it to the Internet and joined my IRC chats. I was able to install GIMP, the Linux version of Photoshop. I never really liked the GIMP GUI though. I was quite proud of myself.

The Startup Dot Com/CLEC Years

In November of 1999, Tony and I moved to Tampa to look for work after we graduated with our two-year degrees in computers. I got an interview with a .COM, Vitalcast. The job description listed ASP (Active Server Pages), so I went out and bought an ASP for Dummies book and started reading it.

I had never interviewed before, so I was very nervous. I was only 19. I bought a pantsuit at Ross. During the interview, Dave Schlageter, an avid cyclist and former IBM employee, was very impressed by my study of C programming. Then after asking me a variety of softball questions, he brought me in to meet Victoria Romero Lara. She would be my supervisor. Victoria, a former basketball player from Spain, had short jet black hair and an exotic Spanish accent. She asked what experience I had doing web development, so I pulled up my personal site. She was impressed by my hand-written rollovers! Then I decided to go out on a limb and show her my Matrix fan page. She went crazy with excitement. It turned out she was a huge Matrix fan. We totally hit it off. They hired me!

I worked ten hours every day while at Vitalcast. I became an expert at ASP and started writing Visual Basic COM Objects too. I learned a great deal about windows servers, IIS, and how to register COM Objects.
Among many things I learned from Vitalcast:

1. **Business plans are important**. They didn't have one, and they went out of business six months after I joined.

2. **Don't panic**. My co-worker Dave Smith and I were updating our production server and something went wrong. I started freaking out and he simply said, "Panicking doesn't help. Staying calm will let your mind keep working to find a solution." I've used that advice on many occasions since then.

3. **Keep in touch and never burn your bridges**. Victoria and I are still friends to this day. It's more important to keep a friendly relationship, even if the company you work for goes under and they have to lay you off. Your previous employers are the most important help to get a new job. You need them to give you a good recommendation.

When I left Vitalcast six months later, I was an expert with ASP, COM Objects, IIS and VB. When they called us into a big conference room to let us know that we were all laid off, I was much better off than I had been six months earlier. I felt nothing but grateful. Getting my second job was a bit more difficult. I interviewed at a few places 'till I got hired on a one-month contract to do HTML at a hosting firm called Digital Chainsaw. I drove daily from north Tampa to St. Petersburg to the Digital Chainsaw office, about one hour and 15 minutes away.

They hired me to code one simple website. They gave me word docs and I had to translate them into HTML. I created a spreadsheet to track the 30 pages that needed to be coded. The manager showed amazement at my organization. I was only 20 at this time. I thought it was funny. I finished coding after three days. This was a big problem because they had hired me for a 30 day contract.

"Can I have another project to do?" I asked.

"No, that's all we had for you. Just relax and surf the web." the manager said.

"Please, I can't just sit here" I replied.

"Well the only thing we have to code is ColdFusion projects." The manager replied. "Then give me a book and I'll learn it."

So I did. I spent the day reading and trying to code in ColdFusion. It didn't make any sense at all. Finally, at 4:50, I realized ColdFusion is just like HTML. It uses tags to do loops and database pulls. Once it clicked I wrote up a Hello World program and showed it to my boss.

"See, I can do this." I beamed.

"Cool! Tomorrow I'll give you a project to do." he said.

The following day, first thing in the morning, I heard frantic voices across the large programming den that all of us geeks sat in. I walked over to see what was going on.

"Does anyone know ASP?" The project manager was asking.

"Yeah, I did ASP at my last job." I said.

Everyone gathered around excited. I was the only one who knew how to do it, and it was an important project. I quickly got busy working on it. They renewed my contract every month for a few months, and then rolled me over into an employee slot. I worked there for two years before a large corporation bought them and closed them down.

But while I worked there, I coded a variety of project types. My management knew they could throw anything my way, and I'd figure out how to do it. I wrote automation scripts so that customers could order online, and the scripts would automatically set up their FTP and websites for both UNIX and Windows web servers. I also set up a chat room so that our tech support could chat with our customers. That was a fun project because I had to make the chat room censor all cuss words. I had to create a text file with all the words I wanted it to replace with special characters. Since I am not much of a curser, I had a hard time coming up with all the possible words to include in my file.

The two memorable things I learned at Digital Chainsaw were:

1. Your **attitude will be the difference between keeping a job or losing a job**. Have the will to make your ideas reality, and follow through. Be willing to learn new things.

2. **Audio books turn a long boring drive into a mind expanding time**.

During those two years I finished LOTR, Atlas Shrugged, lots and lots of Asimov's books, and much more.

After Digital Chainsaw went out of business, I got a job at Z-Tel Communications Inc. Z-Tel was created after the 1996 Telecommunications Act, which enabled the reselling of local phone services by competitive local exchange carriers (CLECs). I went in as an ASP developer, but within two months, I was writing JSP pages. Within six months I was writing JAVA J2EE objects. I worked there for three years, and made a few more friends at Z-Tel. I worked for a businessman who I'll call Bob. When he interviewed me, I asked him a lot of questions about Z-Tel's business plan. I drilled him for a while before agreeing to work at Z-Tel. He later would often tell me that I had more business smarts than most of the folks in the company. My proudest moment at Z-Tel was when I wrote my own shopping cart. We did some fun things with Java and XML. We would pass objects as XML around our state machine. I first learned the importance of architecture at Z-Tel. I worked with some very smart folks who taught me a great deal about how to construct software.

The main things I learned from my experience at Z-Tel:

1. Business plans are critical
2. Spend more time designing and less time coding and testing.

Verizon

After Z-Tel laid me off due to their failing business model, I decided to go back to college full time and get my four-year degree in computer science. My two-year AS in computer programming didn't transfer cleanly into USF, so I had been taking pre-reqs classes one by one for about a year at the community college before I got laid off from Z-Tel. I got two months' severance from Z-Tel, and I loved my time off. I started running and trained for a Triathlon. Just as I was getting comfy at home, two weeks before my severance ran out, I got a call from a contracting company who was trying to place someone at Verizon as a Java developer.

When they told me they would pay for my college, I decided to take the interview, and I got the job. I worked for three months doing data analysis for a very complex system before the moment that changed my life happened. One day my boss Kevin Fouche, an adept sailor, gave all of us developers business cases for a variety of projects so that we could help write up the summary and benefits.

The business case I was given was called TIGER, Tool to Identify and Generate ESG Revenue. TIGER, a rules engine, mined existing customer data to identify customers who were ready to be upsold to better services. I liked the project so much that Kevin put me in charge of the entire thing. I was given two developers and a tester. I interviewed sales folks from around the country to understand how they were currently identifying customers to "upsell." I created the project plan, the design docs and diagrams, and performed code reviews. It was a fantastic experience. And I got a taste for doing architecture and requirements with business clients.

Unfortunately, the team had to cut resources, and I found out that I was going to get laid off. I met James Horianopoulos, a towering man who moonlighted as a DJ by night, in the hall one day and we had become friends. We had gone to lunch a few times before I found out that I needed to look for a new job. I asked James if his team was hiring, and he said yes. He recommended me to his boss and sent my resume over. Soon I had an interview there with their team. They said I was overqualified, but because I wanted to do more requirements and work with clients, I took the job. The pay was VERY low.

Working as a systems requirements analyst wasn't as sexy as it first sounded. I had fallen in love with working with clients and developing a tool to make their lives better. But as a systems requirements analyst, I was just writing down what others told me to write.

After a month I was ready to quit. Then I got assigned to the wild, Wild West of systems, particularly an inventory system for Layer 3 services. For the first few weeks the manager, Anurag Mishra, didn't like that I was setting up calls and making decisions, but after a few more months of working for him, he started to trust me. After a year of working closely with him, he would let me make all the design decisions for the system.

I also got very involved in VOIP at this time. I met my hero Danilo Puseljic, who was a VOIP architect. Danilo, an assiduous, patient architect first showed me what an enterprise end-to-end architect did. Danilo, a talk lanky Yugoslavian, always gave me time as I began to study everything he did, and asked him lots of questions. Soon he gave me small projects to design.

At the same time I met another hero and mentor, Peter Stein. Peter, whose distinctive booming New Jersey brogue is recognized by anyone who's ever talked to him before, took me under his wing and let me be very involved in the architecture process. Peter's sense of humor kept even the most grueling requirements session light-hearted.

This is something that will happen to you: You will have to do a job before you get paid for it. Remember at this point I am making very, very little money. But doing architectures really helped me have the confidence for the interview, which I got a few months later for a full-time architecture position at Verizon. Peter recommended me to Srinivasa Kalapala, the manager of an architecture department. He joined one of the calls I conducted, and listened in on how I managed the meeting and led the discussion. He hired me, and I was a full architect only one year after I decided to become an architect! Srini, a thoughtful manager, built a team within the next few years. During that time I wrote "Best Practices," a learning aid for new team members.

I worked on 25 separate projects each year for the next few years. I can say that it's absolutely the best job.

Key lessons from Verizon:
1. Don't hesitate to do a **job** before you get **paid**.
2. Do **extra work** that others **don't** want to do.

3. Ask people to **mentor** you.

Part 3: Steps to become a Software Architect

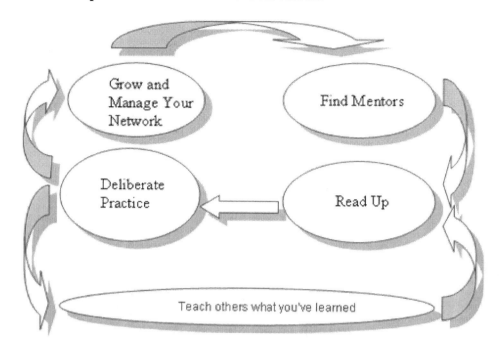

Figure 2- Figure Infinity System

Grow your Network

As developers, we love coding. Give us a requirement and we will bang it out. We want a technical problem so we can create an algorithm to solve it. We will optimize and refine our code. We will create an efficient sorting method. Our fingers ache for the keyboard and a good song to code to.

BUT, if we want to reach the next level of our career, architecture, we need to poke our head out of the cube and meet others. OMG! Did she really say that I have to meet other humans in 3rd space??? Yes I did!

Growing your network by meeting people in your industry will allow you to create connections.

How to prepare for meeting: Make sure you are dressed in the proper attire for the event. Make sure your clothes are clean and you smell nice, not too much fragrance. Grooming is important when you're trying to make a good first impression.

Where do you meet them? If your company is big enough that you don't know everyone yet, you could meet someone at the "water cooler," or at a company party. The bigger your company, the more important it is that you know everyone that you can. This includes peers, leads, managers, directors and executives. Knowing others and having a great reputation in their eyes are key to your success. Why do you need to know the leaders in other parts of your company? Because if something happens in your organization that requires you to seek a new job, you can apply to another group. This has happened to me several times in Verizon. Also, when something is going on, you can find out the inside story through your network.

You should also meet new people at conventions and meet-up groups. These folks can help you find jobs, and also help you when you need to hire.

What do you do? Make eye contact. Smile. Shake their hand and introduce yourself.

What do you say? People are always interested in themselves, so the best way to make a good impression with someone is to ask them about themselves. Ask them what they are working on, what languages they use, or where they went to college. Just keep asking and listening, and be sure to remember what they say.

How do you create a lasting connection? The better your communication skills are, the easier it will be for you to create a lasting connection. Communication skills are making the right amount of eye contact, not too much and not too little. People who can't make eye contact are thought of as being dishonest, and are generally not trusted. First impressions are the only impressions that matter at a convention/meet-up where people are deciding quickly who will be a useful connection.

Make sure you remember the details of their projects and skills and any other personal details. (Jot down notes later to help you remember.) Give them your card. Get their email address and phone number. Ask them if you can look them up on Linkedin.com. Talk about the next meeting you might both attend. If you really hit it off, then ask them for coffee.

My own network helped me in many ways. I'll share a few.

I met a swing dancer who was also a computer scientist professor. A few months later I was working on an abstract for a submission for a conference and I had him review it. He helped tighten it up and it was accepted.

James Horianopoulos who I met in the hall at the office helped me get the job as a Systems Analyst at Verizon.

One day as I left my orthopedist's office I struck up a conversation with a man also on his way out. We quickly became friends and he and his wife stayed with my family on their trip around the US in an RV.

Most of those who helped me edit this book I met in chance meetings at events I attended.

The more events and activities your involved in the more chances you have to grow your network. I am involved in Toastmasters, Swing Dancing, book club, improv acting, martial arts, church, besides local developer groups. The wider your networks, the more people you will meet.

Find Mentors

After your network has expanded from 0 to n, you need to decide which of your new connections will be a good mentor. A mentor is someone who will give you counsel on your career and on design decisions. Mentoring can be informal or formal. A formal mentor might be someone your company assigns to you or someone you meet on your own. You have regularly scheduled sessions with them, and progress is carefully tracked. Informal mentors are people whom you trust, and call when you need advice. You might meet with them occasionally to update them on your progress.

Throughout your career you will need a variety of different mentors at each step of your progress. Each mentor will be able to help you to move to the next level, at which point you'll need to find a mentor for the next level up. A mentor should be someone you admire and hope to be like one day.

When choosing a mentor, you need to look at the salient criteria:
1. Their position
2. Their expertise
3. Their personality
4. Their openness to mentoring
5. Their availability
6. Their patience level

Once you've found a few potential mentors, just ask if they are willing to mentor you, and if they say no, be willing to accept that. People may have reasons why they cannot, and you should not take it personally.

If they say yes, then you should determine if you want to have a formal mentoring relationship or an informal relationship. This will mainly depend on their time availability and personality.

The mentoring relationship is the place where you will grow the most. Getting feedback on how you're doing, and learning the best practices can be invaluable. But the most important benefit is that a mentor can support you and recommend you for jobs which are key to getting ahead.

So how many mentors can someone have? I have many, and you can have many mentors as practical. It's best to have a variety of mentors who specialize in different areas so that you can call on them for their specialized advice. Also, you might want to get several opinions on big decisions.

When I have to design something big that I've not done before, I usually call a few folks and discuss it with them. Then I make my own decision after they've given me their opinions.

Your network of trusted mentors will make you a powerful unstoppable force. It's your secret tool for any project or decision you're tackling. It will give you a huge advantage over those developers/architects who try to do everything alone.

Also you will find that you are mentoring others. This will increase your network and your power. You'll learn so much by listening to others' issues and helping them reason through them. You'll find that by being a mentor you learn more than from any other source. You'll be challenged and you will grow.

Read Up

Now that you've grown your network and found trusted mentors, you need to read as much as possible in your areas of specialization. The books/magazines/articles/blogs/forums you should be looking at range from the technical updates in your chosen technology to changes in regulation that impact the business and economic trends of your industry. You should read up on trends that affect the architecture, patterns and tools of your technology if you want to become an effective leader.

The key is the quality of the information you're absorbing. Make sure that the information is worth remembering.

There are three steps to being able to figure out what's going to happen next:

1. Research what happened before (history).
2. Keep up with daily events (news).
3. Learn in depth about what's happening now (documentaries, current events books, podcasts).

The average American reads less than one book a year. They say that if you read 3 books on any subject you will be an expert in that topic. If you can master the power of reading books, you will be heads above everyone around you. Almost all successful people have one thing in common: They read voraciously.

So far in 2011, I've finished about 3 to 4 books a month. My secret for finishing books so quickly is that I listen to books on my iPod. At any given time, I am listening to a book on my iPod, reading several on my Kindle, and several more on paper. I listen to my books whenever I am driving, cooking, showering, cleaning or exercising. When I sit down to eat, or before I go bed, I always read a Kindle book or a paper book.

Many people tell me they don't have time to read. If you fall into this category, then do the following:

1. Create a reading list by asking your mentors, Googling, and looking at the recommended reading from Amazon based on your previous purchases.
2. Make a goal of reading n number of books by x date. Be realistic based on your history, but stretch yourself also.
3. Prioritize your reading list according to those that you absolutely need to finish first
4. Schedule time each day/week to read.

5. When your scheduled time to read starts, turn off your cell phone, TV, audio, and listen to music that allows you to focus. Also block access to your Facebook, email and twitter feed. If you're anything like me, you need to block out distractions in order to read.

6. Write notes on what you learn. Write a blog entry; write a book review on linkedin.com. Make sure that you talk about the book with your mentors and connections to help imbed the things you've learned into your brain.

7. Check the book off your list and move on!

Some good books that I highly recommend are the following:

Title: *The Information*
Author: James Gleick
Why: It covers all the major milestones in the history of computer science
from the perspective of information.

Title: *Software Architecture in Practice*
Author: Len Bass
Why: This book gives lots of tools to use to gather requirements and determine the design of a system.

Title: *The Seven Habits of Highly Effective People*
Author: Steven Covey
Why: Architects are highly effective people. There are many things that can steal our time. Steven reviews the ways that we can stay highly effective.

Title: *Overcoming the Five Dysfunctions of a Team*
Author: Patrick M. Lencioni
Why: You'll need to function effectively in a team.

Title: *Life is a Series of Presentations:*
Eight Ways to Inspire, Inform,
and Influence Anyone,
Anywhere, Anytime
Author: Tony Jeary
Why: Teaches you how to put together a presentation to persuade an audience.

Title: *So What's your Point?*
Author: James C. Wetherbe and Bond Wetherbe
Why: How to persuasively make your point, boost your credibility, overcome objections, avoid misunderstandings, and minimize arguments in your professional and personal communication.

Title: *Death by Meetings*
Author: Patrick M. Lencioni
Why: You'll need to run effective meetings

Title: *Tipping Point*
Author: Malcolm Gladwell
Why: As architects, we are leaders. Thus we need to be influential and create change in our areas of expertise. Gladell gives case histories of how change occurs, which you can use to create the change you want.

Title: *Talent is Overrated*
Author: Geoff Colvin
Why: Exposes the real secret to top performance, which is deliberate practice with coaching.

Title: *Will Power*
Author: John Tierney, Roy Baumeister
Why: Helps you understand the ways to build and use will power, the key to a successful career as an architect.

Title: *Influencer*
Author: Kerry Patterson and others
Why: As architects, we are leaders; thus we need to be influential, and create change in our areas of expertise. Kerry picks up where Gladwell leaves off, and provides the 6 components of influence that need to be considered when creating a change.

Title: *Our Iceberg is Melting*
Author: John Kotter
Why: Step by step for bringing a team thru change.

Title: *Good to Great*
Author: Jim Collins
Why: Explains the essential qualities of an architect: disciplined people, disciplined thoughts and disciplined action.

Title: *Linchpin*
Author: Seth Godin
Why: Architects are the linchpins of projects. They hold the whole thing together. They deliver more than what's expected. Seth does a great job of giving the history of work, and how the future of work looks.

Reading great books will set you apart from others. Once you've read the technical, business, and personal development books, read the classics. These will make you a well-rounded person who will be able to converse more easily with people from different backgrounds. It will make you appreciate life more fully and give you a depth that attracts people. The classics are incredible; yet hardly anyone reads them. But I guarantee you that if you take the time and read them, that effort will do more for your career and overall satisfaction in life than you can imagine. In 2010, I read or listened to one classic a month for the entire year. The following are the ones I finished:

Jan 2010: *Moby Dick* (***) by Herman Melville
Feb 2010: *Great Expectations* (*****) by Charles Dickens
March 2010: *War and Peace* (*****) by Leo Tolstoy
April 2010: *Bleak House* (*****) by Charles Dickens
May 2010: *Alice in Wonderland* (****) by Lewis Caroll
June 2010: *Heart of Darkness* (***) by Joseph Conrad
July 2010: *The Idiot* (***) by Fyodor Dostoyevsky
Aug 2010: *Hamlet* (****) by William Shakespeare
Sept 2010: *Around The World in Eighty Days* (***) by Jules Vern
Oct 2010: *Lord of the Flies* (***) by William Golding
Nov 2010: *Kim* (****) by Rudyard Kipling
Dec 2010: *One day in the Life of Ivan Denisovich* (****) by Aleksandr Solzhenitsyn.

If you can listen to audio books and focus on them, I highly recommend you do so. Otherwise, make sure that you're scheduling time to read. It's crucial for you as an architect to be very well rounded as well as fully versed in all the current events impacting your industry.

Network Management

You've grown your network by adding new people to it, you've identified key folks as your mentors, and you've read up to get a baseline of knowledge. Now its time to manage your network. Each connection you make will grow your network exponentially. In these relationships, you should be identifying two items: What are your connection's goals, and what are their strengths. These two items should help you focus your interactions on how can I help my contacts reach their goals, and how can their strengths help me in mine. But if you do not know how to manage that network, you are not gaining anything. Managing your network includes keeping track of the strengths of each of your contacts, and properly utilizing those strengths when the time comes that you need them. Network management is a competitive advantage for those who take the time to develop the skills. Let's talk about the skills.

The skills are: building trust, personal communication and memory.

Think about the person you trust the most in the whole world. Now think about the person you don't trust. There's a huge difference. In his important book *Speed of Trust* by Stephen M. R. Covey, he asserts that trust impacts the cost and speed of any group. When a survey was taken at a specific office, everyone agreed on who the untrustworthy people were. Are you a trustworthy person? If you are, people will want to let you into their network and help you. If you are not, you need to learn the basic building blocks of trust that *Speed of Trust* shows can help you rebuild trust.

"Trust is the one thing that changes everything." (Stephen M. R. Covey)

The following is a summary of some of the key points from The *Speed of Trust* by Stephen M. R. Covey.

In every situation your priority should be to build trust with those around you. Trust decreases cost and time in any effort. Think about how long it takes to get through airline security now that we can't trust passengers, all as the result of one person who decided to take a bomb on a plane. Extra security boosts the cost of hiring extra security officers, and it takes us an extra hour to get on an airplane instead of the 30 minutes it used to take.

The three ingredients required for trust are:
1. Integrity

2. Intent

3. Competence

Let's ask questions on each aspect:

1. Integrity

Integrity is different from honesty. Honesty suffers through omission, intentionally leaving out information, or through commission, presenting truth in a way that misleads others. Integrity is communicating clearly and making sure the others fully understand the reality of the situation.

2. Intent

Intent is hidden inside a person and can be a cause of speculation. It's best to tell others your intent so that they understand it. Your intent should be win/win, and if it's not then you should examine your assumptions about what's important.

3. Competence

Someone can be sincere, but if they don't have the ability, then they need to recognize that. If you wish to be trustworthy, constantly increase your competence in your area. Delivering results is the fastest way to build trust.

The Speed of Trust is an excellent book that covers how trust impacts relationships and your success, from your family to your company's brand in the market, and how to build trust in each of those domains.

Personal communication is those basic skills of personal interaction that can either make you a person that people seek or someone they avoid. *In the Art of Loving*, Eric Fromm says, "This desire for interpersonal fusion is the most powerful striving in man. It is the most fundamental passion; it is the force which keeps the human race together, the clan, the family, society." (pg 17)

Most of personal communication is not talking, it's listening. Listening is an act of love that will endear you to anyone you meet. It is also one of the hardest things to do. Sometimes someone will be talking to me, and my thoughts are so loud I can't actually hear the person. Also the one taboo that makes some folks so avoidable is their tendency to talk too much and not listen.

We all know folks like this, and sometimes we are related to them. If you do not have a sensor that says, "I've been talking a lot, let me stop and listen now," then you need to force yourself to listen and ask questions. It's a muscle that you need to exercise. After your conversation with a person, think on it, and repeat parts that are important. Identify the core details of what was covered in your conversation. What is important to them? What are their goals?

Your memory system can be internal stored, or you can create an external inventory system. If you do not have a good memory, you will definitely suffer in network management. Usually you have to have both internal and external augmentation. Write a few important points about a person on their business card when they hand it to you. Also, put all the business cards in an inventory system. Either scan or file them. You can get as elaborate as you want on this item. As soon as possible, look up your new contact on Facebook and LinkedIn and add them to your inventory system.

I've received several jobs as a result of people connecting with me on Facebook, people who I've only briefly met in person. Don't underestimate the importance of the social media connections. These platforms allow you to keep up with your new connection, and easily contact them when you need to.

Now that you have identified their goals and strengths, you need to utilize those folks in your network that can help you, as you help them. This is a skill that may come naturally, or you might need to manually review your contacts to see which one matches the need, or do both.

Utilize your network effectively in two ways. The first way to use your network is by connecting your contacts with others that will help them get to their goals. Often I'll be in a conversation with someone, and they will mention that they are putting on an event or doing a project, and one of my connection's names will pop into my mind. I'll then send my connection that information for them to follow up.

The second way is to use your contacts for your own goals. When you have a challenge, you can reach out to the person with the closest strengths in that area and ask them for help. But you can only do this if you've built some trust with each other. Make sure that you don't take from your contacts without giving back. Otherwise you'll soon have no connections.

Don't forget to keep your network current. Drop your contacts a line of communication as often as you think is necessary to keep up. Find out what's new with them. Social media again makes this very easy.

Network management is the completive advantage for knowledgeable workers, especially architects. Make a determined effort to add network management skills to your profile to achieve success.

Deliberate Practice

The goal is to be an expert architect who can handle any design challenge that comes up, but how do you get there? To be an expert, Malcolm Gladwell says you need 10,000 hours of experience. Experience is nothing more than practice. Now we can get a little fancy with the math and say that every hour you spend coding can be counted towards your 10k, but I think we need to be a little more specific.

Architecture is an act of design. We all design when we code. Sometimes we design for five minutes, sometimes for a few months. The process of designing is the part that counts towards the 10k hours. If you are currently a developer, then when you are designing, you are moving towards your goal.

The challenge is getting more and more challenging projects to design. You should be seeking new challenges to expand your mind. There are so many types of software architecture, but they all depend on a few of the same basic principles to complete. First you must understand the requirements of the system.

To find the requirements, you must answer the same "ility" questions: reliability, testability and so on. These are covered in the excellent book *Software Architecture in Practice* by Len Bass. Once you understand the requirements of the system, you need to move to identifying the inputs and outputs.

As you can see, you can practice the thinking along these paths even when you are a developer, and probably already do so every day. When you're architecting a small program, you will break the general requirement into functions and procedures. You will define each function's input and output. This is exactly the same approach you'd take if you were architecting the engine management system for a hybrid car. You'd break the overall requirements into modules, and define inputs and outputs for each. As an architect you will design how these inputs and outputs flow between the modules, including sequence, frequency, attributes, data types and conditions.

If you are in a position where you can architect with more complex programs, you would do the same exact steps. The exact steps in doing an architecture don't really change, but the challenges of working on more complex systems grow exponentially. When you are working on an existing system that you are only upgrading, it's highly unlikely to be fully documented, which means you will have a host of unknowns to work with. When you add in multiple departments, you will then need to deal with political issues. Add in distribution, and you'll need to examine architecture patterns to ensure reliability.

The other day I was in a mall buying some hand soap, and their credit card validating module was down. Their software's architecture allowed them to call a number and validate the credit card on the phone, then manually enter the confirmation number into their software. This architecture decision was driven by the requirement of allowing a manual confirmation of the credit card validation to be entered. The system had to allow for both input from an API and a user.

The main goal is that you start practicing architecture today. Start positioning yourself to do more design at work each day. Let your manager know your goals so he or she can help you.

Outside work, you can practice architecture by creating your own systems, or finding an organization where you can volunteer. My work for the graphics group, creating web applications, helped me get my first job. You can find an organization that needs software help and volunteer there.

At a volunteer-type organization, you will learn all the skills you need to become a great architect. The organization's leadership might not realize that software will be the answer to their challenges, so you need to listen carefully to their needs and then put together a holistic proposal. In that type of organization, where people come and go, they will want something maintainable and inexpensive. Make sure you listen and answer all their questions before you start designing.

Your 10k hours won't come easy, but if you open your eyes to the design opportunities around you, you can start working towards your goal. Between focusing on the design side at work and volunteering somewhere, you'll soon have enough experience to expand your resume sufficiently to justify application for your first pure software architecture job. Just make sure the folks you work for write you great recommendation letters.

But what if your architectures aren't perfect? Let's look at what happens when you go after the perfect architecture. The difference between the right architecture and the perfect architecture is the difference between finishing a project, and being fired for never finishing the project. You need to seek an architecture that meets the purpose of the project. That includes timeliness.

The main thing you want to avoid, as an architect, is analysis paralysis. You know paralysis happens when you keep searching for the absolute perfect solution to the problem. What you need to do is to find the solution that meets the requirements. When you can't find the solution that meets all requirements, then you need to negotiate trade-offs.

Another technique is to find a solution that meets most of the requirements right now, and can be upgraded later when a better solution can be developed to meet all the requirements.

A recent project required a quick search through a large database, but our team only had the technology for a slow search. We went through several meetings trying to see how we could speed up the search using standard SQL performance enhancers. We soon realized we were in analysis paralysis due to the inexperience and inability of our team to write a powerful search engine. The clients would not accept a final project with the performance we were getting from the current search, but we didn't have the expertise to create something faster. We finally found a resource within our organization who developed a powerful search engine that we could leverage, but couldn't be able to integrate into our system till much later in the project. That's when we had to negotiate a trade-off with the clients. "We will give you a slow search now, but later we will be able to meet your need for a fast search." They agreed. Perfect architecture is less important than meeting most of the requirements, and negotiating where needed.

Of course there is always the situation where the ideal solution cannot be found. This is the point where you have to become an engineer. You have to just find a solution that can meet the highest priority requirements. To ensure that you know which requirements are the highest priorities, review them with your client and stakeholders. Make sure they agree and understand the situation fully.

How do we actually go about finding a solution and architecture? This is where creativity comes in, and architecture is pure creation: knowing your restraints and your restrictions is part of the process.

Let's review seven steps to create architecture. Number one, you need to list all the things that are known by making a mental map. Try writing the items on a white board, or create a PowerPoint that lists them through a brain dump of the different things that you know. You should write constraints, data that you need, and sources of data. Here is an example of a mental map for a calculator.

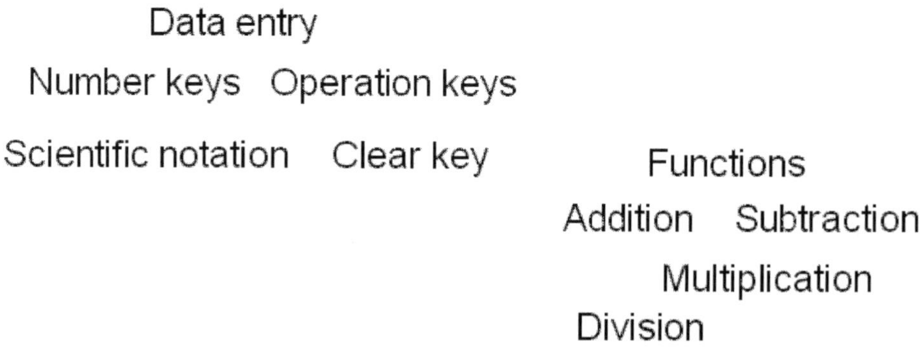

Data entry
Number keys
Operation keys
Scientific notation
Clear key
Functions
Addition
Subtraction
Multiplication
Division

Figure 3: Calculator Mental Map

Step two, now that you have all the things that you need in your mental map, you can start drawing a new box and line diagram to show a use case with the data flow. To describe the data coming from the data entry, you can draw a stick figure with a line to a box labeled GUI. From there draw a line to another box with the label function. The following is an example.

Number keys
Operation keys
Key Pad
Display
GUI
Number + number
Answer
Addition Function

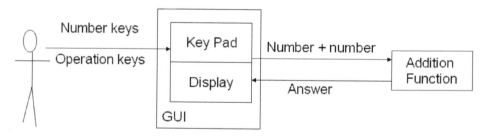

Figure 4: Calculator Addition Use Case

Third, after drawing one use case or scenario, you can start thinking about different scenarios and list those out. Once you have identified different scenarios, start creating a list of all the different use cases.

Use cases for calculator:

Addition

Subtraction

Multiplication

Division

Fourth, now that you have a list of high-level use cases, you can start creating architecture proposals. It's good to create several alternative proposals for a couple reasons. First, it allows you to think freer since you know that each architecture is just one of a few. You feel less pressure, which invites creativity. Second it will allow your team to think more widely about the solution, and give you more feedback. For each architecture, ask yourself the following questions, and make design decisions based on them. How many modules do you need? What data does each model receive? What kind of layers are best suited? Should modules be physically distributed? What type of database model is going to work the best for your system? How could you meet the requirements of speed? What technologies will work the best for your requirements?

This is when you need to consider technology decisions that are already decided. For instance, your company has an Oracle contract, thus your database will be Oracle. Further, you're production support has requirements on the server type, and doesn't allow you to select anything you want. Thus, many decisions may already be done, and you will need to make sure your requirements can fit into those constraints. In the rare situation that you're creating something completely from scratch, make decisions based on technology and cost.

Fifth, now that you have several alternatives, start documenting the pros and cons of each alternative architecture. PowerPoint works well when giving a presentation, or you could use a Word document. Lay the solutions out before the team. Reviewing your architecture in progress with the team is important for a couple of reasons. First, it alerts your awareness of issues early on, which will avoid those issues later. Second, it allows the team to be part of the solution, which is important for their buy–in to the solution. Don't get emotional. Encourage each person providing feedback so that it will keep coming. You'll find that the best architecture is somewhere in the middle of the ones you created. The team can help you stitch together the best architecture from the elements you provided.

Step six is dealing with external data received and sending data to external systems. First let's look at receiving external data. To get external data, we need an interface. External might mean outside the company, or just from an existing system inside the company. Let's walk though the thought process behind external data. When you realize you need a piece of data that you do not have, you need to list your data requirements. How fresh does the data need to be? How often do you need the data refreshed? What is the "golden source" of the data? Golden source means the source that created the data. Once you've looked at each of those data requirements, and then list the possible sources for the data. Determine which of those sources best meets the requirements.

Sending data to external systems will be first recognized as a requirement of the system, and later other systems will come to ask for the data when they find out you have it. Reporting, billing, and accounting are examples of systems that will want your new data, and you will need to write requirements for each of them. To write the requirements, ask how often do they need the data? Can the data be sent in batch, or is it needed in real time? What fields do they require?

Once you've answered these questions, you can start looking at what technology they already use. Cost of developing a brand new type of interface infrastructure might not be feasible, so you might need to work with the externals' way of interfacing.

Let's look at the politics of interfaces. Sometimes you have a choice over which system you are going to use for the data you need. When this is the case, you should consider a few items. First consider technology. If one of the external systems is a mainframe, you might have a difficult time getting the data out of it, so you might want to select a different external system. The second item you should consider is politics. The political structure will come into play if there is an external system that has great speed, and has great data quality. But you may find that the director of that system is a difficult person to deal with. You may not want to deal with that person and instead go to another system where you get along really well the director. You want a system that has management that gets along very well, and has a smooth trusting relationship with your own management. This means that you are aligned on vision, technology, release schedules, support, documentation types and testing. These things end up being a big pain if you don't have alignment. Making sure that you can rely on the external systems for your critical data is a really important part of architecture. When you make a decision to put your critical data in another system, you are obviously taking a risk because that system's management might change. Hopefully, if you have alignment on most items, even if one or two elements change, you still have the other pieces.

Let's discuss IDs for a few minutes. If you are designing a brand-new system, and you can create a single-source identifier for your records that is well-known, then save yourself a world of trouble by promptly making a few design decisions. The format of the ID is extremely important. Don't build logic into your ID because you think you'll only need 500. Those kinds of decisions will very quickly bite you because eventually you'll need 10 thousand of them, and you're stuck with some kind of format that prevents you from getting 10 thousand IDs. If you think this doesn't happen, you're wrong. Look at IP addresses.

Of course, I told you already, don't over-think everything, but definitely try to make sure that your design allows for more than what you think is going to be its limit. Create a design that allows you to expand in ways that you might need to expand. Often, you end up creating a code that really is going to put you in a corner, and I strongly recommend you don't allow that to happen.

Once you have identified the different systems with the best data and the best political status, review the interfaces at a high level with your team, and see what they say. They may find issues such as "the data the other system is providing isn't as fresh as you need it to be." Your team might also identify that you missed an interface. It's better that you find out now rather than later.

Now that you have both internal and external interfaces determined at a high level, you can write a detailed interface document, or you can have a business analyst (BA) write one, depending on the structure of your team.

The seventh and final step is to package up your final solution, which your team approved with all your interfaces, and draw a high-level design. This document will show the high-level modules of your system, and the interfaces they have with external systems. This document should have several views, including the big picture with very little data shown, and close ups of the internal modules with the key data between each, as well as the external systems with the key data between their and your modules.

Do a final review with your team, and with your upper management, and make sure everyone understands and feels comfortable with your design.

Teach Others What You Learn

Ever meet someone who has "plateaued?" I am an avid swing dancer. I often see dancers who've reached a level of competence, but never grow any further. It's like they decided, "Yep, I am good enough and that's all I need to do to get by." They fail to realize that getting by is not the goal. The goal is constant improvement. One key way to avoid lasting plateaus is to remember the essential techniques, and to keep learning and teaching.

First, document the essential techniques that made you a successful architect in the beginning. When we are actively growing in an area, we are identifying the essential techniques that make others successful. We are sponges and driven to find out why those ahead of us are so good. Your senses are keen in the beginning, which later can become dull due to apathy or self confidence. This is the time that you need to be documenting each essential technique.

Each time you have an "Aha" moment, record it in a blog or journal. This is not a diary that little girls keep, this is an architecture journal. One that you will go back and read regularly to remind yourself of the essential techniques that made you successful. When you find a technique that works, note it down. When you discover something that didn't work, note it down. Record important quotes you read or hear. Sketch your designs and then any comments on them.

These notes are not just techniques; they are a documentation of your passion. Later in your career, go back and read your notes. These will remind you of the little things that made you successful. These little improvements usually are related to the basics that you discover early in your career. Just as a swing dancer needs to focus on connection with their partner while listening to the music, an architect needs to focus on connecting with his/her team and listening to the clients. When you move along in your career, don't allow yourself to get distracted by the politics and forget those essential skills.

Writing down your ideas is a good start, but the next step is to share those. Sharing what you learn will accentuate the lessons in your own mind. Sharing can come in several flavors. You can either teach a group or mentor an individual. You can also write a blog, article or book!

Start sharing with a mentee. Find a mentee who has the passion to learn what you know. Connect with that person and review the things you've learned. When you teach them, your own passion will be reignited. Dole out your wisdom gently as to not overwhelm your mentee. Set up regular sessions with him or her. I have several mentees who I work with regularly. Watching them succeed is very rewarding.

Next, move to small group teaching sessions. Where can you teach? You can speak to a group within your own company, or to a group in a local university, or even to a software meetup group.

At your own company, you can set up a small brown bag lunch at your office and invite those who you think are on their way to becoming an architect. Start teaching with an overview; then have a series of follow-up lessons on different subjects.

In 2010 I taught a different session every month at Verizon. I had the support of my executive director, which definitely helped. I'd pick a subject, and then narrow it to something I could cover in the one-hour session. I'd write my presentation as a 4D outline (see best practices on giving a presentation at the end of this book), then create my PowerPoint. I spent quite a bit of time creating the curriculum each month, but it was very rewarding when I saw the faces smiling during my sessions. I learned so much in 2010.

At the beginning of 2011, I started The Architects Club at Verizon. We meet twice a month, and have three 8- to 10-minute speeches followed by five minutes of questions. I give a speech every once in a while, and I get the benefit of hearing a lot of great speeches by colleagues. I've also made progress in setting up clubs at the other Verizon campuses.

Teaching will reinforce all the lesson content in your own mind, and also help you in other aspects of becoming an even better architect. You become well known in your company as a leader. You will grow your network. Other passionate people will find you and want to add you to their network. Doors will open.

Don't ignore this important step. If you do, you will lose out on so many important opportunities. The people who I meet at my architecture sessions at my office are invaluable to me. If you are deathly afraid of public speaking, then join a Toastmasters Club to get over it. As an architect, you will be giving lots of presentations in your career. You better become very good at it. It is better to overcome your fear and become a persuasive speaker before you get the chance to give that huge presentation to the CIO about your amazing solution that will earn you fame and glory for years to come.

Be certain of this: You will definitely have to give presentations as an architect, so you might as well love it and be very good at it.

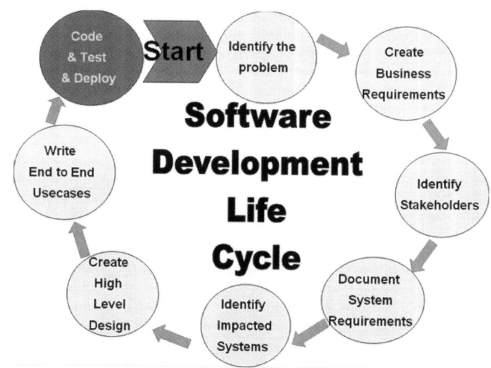

Figure 5: Software Development Life Cycle

The *software development life cycle* is so easily grasped, and yet you can spend your lifetime trying to execute it perfectly. Developing software can keep you challenged and entertained for your whole life. As an architect, you will be involved in most of the cycle. Because, as an architect, you have the end-to-end view of the business processes, you can assist in identifying problems and creating business requirements. Partnering with business is crucial for you and your company's success. The architect is a leader, and there's no hiding. You are the expert, and you will be sought out at every step of a project's life cycle. So let's look into the different areas of SDLC.

Identify the Problem

As the Subject Matter Expert, or SME, you will be the first person that the business comes to for discussions about any change to the system. You will know when something is not working. On one project, the system generated a monthly report that gave all the records that were missing fields. When we looked into it, we found that the records that were missing fields occurred because of another system. Instead of spending a lot of time curing the results of the missing data, we decided to create the feed. This type of analysis is something that you as the Architect must do. You must identify root causes of issues, and let the business know what they are, either when they come asking, or when you feel motivated to tell them.

Architects lead change efforts. Sometimes they also initiate them by creating a business case. Most companies have a business case lifecycle. This is the time each year that companies analyze all the business cases that their employees recommend. If you have a great idea on how to save money, you can write a business case to have it implemented. A business case shows the benefits of your idea and the costs to implement. Whole books have been written on how to write an excellent business case. I've written at least one business case for work, and several for leadership projects.

Create and Approve Business Requirements

Once a business case is approved, business requirements are documented. These are high level descriptions of how the software should work, including functionality, usability and reliability. Author Len Bass's excellent book, *Software Architecture in Practice,* also emphasizes that most business requirements overlook the two most important aspects of software: testability and modifiability. As an architect you should make the business consider these factors as well as the functionality they want to use.

I've been involved in or written several business requirements documents, and I highly recommend that you as the architect become involved in the requirements process for the following reasons.

First, one reason you need to be deeply involved in the creation of the business requirements is to ensure that the requirements are *clear.* Frequently a business will want to get away with minimal descriptions of their requirements. This leads to rework when the users realize that the project is not what they needed. I've seen this happen so many times that I must really impress you with this need for clarity. You need to read the requirements, and talk through them with the clients to make sure you clearly understand what's being asked. Then have the requirements reflect that clear understanding. If you've ever taken a literary class in college where you had to interpret a poem or story, you'll know that English is very subjective. What you don't want in a software project is every developer interpreting the business requirements in their own way.

Second, another reason you need to be deeply involved in the creation of the business requirements is to ensure that the requirements are *complete*. Make sure that you get all the qualities documented. Len Bass's list includes the following:
Availability
Modifiability
Testability
Usability
Performance
Security

Before you sign off on the requirements, make sure they touch on each of these areas.

Thirdly, you need to be deeply involved in the creation of the business requirements to ensure that you fully understand the *intent* of the system. When you are translating the business requirements to the high-level design, you need to keep the intent of the system foremost in your mind. And there is no better way to get deeply familiar with the intent than to spend a few weeks with the clients and users going through their requirements.

Identify Stakeholders

The changes in or creation of a system will impact people inside the company and outside the company. These people are called stakeholders. Make sure you know all the stakeholders in a project. Many times when a project starts, all the stakeholders aren't involved, and this leads to disaster later when their requirements are not considered during the business requirements gathering stage. Also you need to create a good relationship with each of the stakeholders. Make sure they know that you want to create a system that will benefit each of them. Give them your contact info so that they can call with any concerns.

Document System Requirements

System requirements describe the way the system will function in detail. They are written by business analysts, requirements analysts, or developers. For instance, DSR's will describe what happens when a button is clicked. They will give field level details. They will describe the interfaces between systems.

Identify Impacted Systems

In a larger company any new effort will impact existing systems, and the architect's job is to identify each of those systems and the types of impacts they should expect. The requirements for each impacted system need to be documented. It's best to get the system architect involved in reviewing and writing about each impact to their system. Impacted system owners often take a real interest in the overall effort, so keep their architects and leads in the loop on developments.

Create High-Level Design

Finally it's time to write the high-level design. The "High-Level Design" and "Use Cases" are your main deliverables. The rest of the time you are a subject matter expert, leading and consulting throughout the balance of the project. The high-level design can take many forms. See my chapter on Diagrammatic VS Text.

End-to-End Use Cases

Use cases are fantastic ways of describing each high-level function that the system performs. They take the high-level design and break it into scenarios. Making sure you cover all the necessary scenarios is the trick. For example, I was working on a VoIP product a few years ago. We broke it into the top-level use cases, which were install, disconnect, and modify.

Then we broke each of those down into variations such as Install Product with Feature Set 1. Etc. We ended up with 108 use cases based on those variations. Then we broke the product up into geographic regions based on the type of hardware in each area of the country. The goal is to get a use case as specific as possible without having a lot of "if, then's" in it.

Code, Test & Deploy

This final step is for you and the developers to write the actual code; then the test team tests; the clients perform User Acceptance Testing or UAT; and the code is put into the production system or shipped as the case may be. Architects have a small role as consultants during this phase of the development life cycle.

Requirements

Gathering and documenting excellent business requirements take skill and effort. In this chapter, we will review the tactical way you need to run your business requirements sessions. Tactics can be broken up into two sections: first, planning the sessions and second, running the meeting.

Planning starts with identifying all the participants. Usually the stakeholders in the project will be invited, as well as a team to write the requirements. Excellent business requirements writers should be excellent wordsmiths, listeners, intuitive and patient. It's preferable that they have experience in the subject area, but not strictly needed.

You need a facilitator. The facilitator will keep the meeting on track. They will time discussions and make sure you don't spend more than the allotted time on each topic. Also, make sure that you have a subject matter expert present from each impacted area focused on the work.

Now that you have your team, you need to create a realistic agenda. Allow enough time for each section, but realize you will have to adjust during the meeting as sections require more or less time.

I highly recommend meeting physically in one place instead of using a conference call. Select a room big enough for all the participants. Make sure the room has network connectivity.

Now we move to running your meeting. Discipline, time consciousness, and clarity must reign during the running of the session. I've seen requirements sessions go very badly if these three are not kept at the forefront. Let's look at two examples of requirements sessions, one run poorly and one well.

John arrives late to the 9:00 am meeting at 9:10. He has an agenda that he has not shared with anyone. He opens it up on the overhead. His agenda has timed subject matters, as follows:
9 to 9:30 Ordering
9:30 to 9:45 Billing
9:45: to 10:00 Credit check
10:00 to 10:30 Shipping
10:30 to 11:00 Inventory resupply
11:00 to 11:30 Bar coding
11:30 to 12:00 Storage tracking

12:00 to 1:00 Lunch
1:00 to 1:20 Mass uploads
1:20 to 1:45 Inventory reports
1:45 to 2:00 Customer record
2:00 to 2:30 Customer search
2:30 to 3:00 Customer report
3:00 to 3:30 Accounts payable
4:00 to 4:30 Accounts payable report
4:30 to 6:00 External Interfaces

Sam: "John you are missing the section on Returns."

John: "Oh, I guess we can do that during lunch time."

Sam: "Ok, I guess."

It's now 9:20

John: "Ok everyone, we are starting on ordering."

Everyone chimes in but John doesn't write any notes. They discuss all the things they want for about 30 minutes. The time allotted was 30 minutes.

John: "Ok, so it's been 30 minutes, so let me write this stuff down."

He spends about 15 minutes writing what they said, and they just have to repeat it.

It's now 10:05

John: "I guess lets move to billing."

Tom: "Billing reminds me of the time I went fishing with my uncle in North Carolina...."

Tom launches into a story and John doesn't do anything to stop him. Tom's story takes 5 minutes.

John: "Thanks for the story, Tom. So, billing. What do you guys want for billing?"

It's now 10:10

They talk about billing for 20 minutes. John had scheduled 15 minutes for billing. Then John decides to write it down for 10 minutes.

It's now 10:40.

John: "Now we need to talk about credit check."

Sarah: "I am worried about our credit checking service. I think it's not working. I put my cousin in there, and she passed, and I know that's wrong."

Sarah goes on about the credit checking service itself, and others chime in. John does nothing to stop their red herring conversation, or even put it in the parking lot as an item to follow up on.

When Sarah finished, it's 11:00

John: "Ok, let's talk about credit check requirements."

They talk about the requirements for 20 minutes; then John documents them for 15 minutes.

John: "It's now 11:35, so let's talk about shipping."

Several key people complain they need a break, so they wait about 15 minutes for everyone to come back. Now it's 11:50

Everyone asks to have a lunch break.

The meeting is now several hours behind. People flew in to make it to this meeting from all over the country. They are flying out tomorrow. John will never be able to make up for it.

What are the things that John did wrong? List as many as you can before reading the answers below.

John's serious mistakes:

1. He didn't publish the agenda before the meeting.
2. He showed up late.
3. He was unrealistic, giving no breaks, and then trying to add in the lunch time item.
4. He didn't stop irrelevant topics from being discussed.
5. He didn't put items in the parking lot that needed their own meeting.
6. He didn't have draft requirements already gathered that he could just review with the team.
7. He didn't write anything down during the discussion. As requirements were mentioned, he should have written them down, and then asked everyone to verify his notes.

Now let's look at a good example.

Susan sends out the agenda early. She's told that she is missing returns, and she adds it. Here's her agenda:

9:00 to 9:15 Ordering
9:15 to 9:30 Billing
9:30 to 9:45 Credit check
9:45 to 10:00 Break
10:00 to 10:15 Shipping
10:15 to 10:30 Returns

10:30 to 10:45 Inventory resupply
10:45 to 11:00 Break
11:00 to 11:30 Bar coding
11:30 to 12:00 Storage tracking
12:00 to 1:00 Lunch
1:00 to 1:20 Mass uploads
1:20 to 1:45 Inventory reports
1:45 to 2:00 Break
2:00 to 2:15 Customer record
2:15 to 2:30 Customer search
2:30 to 2:45 Customer report
2:45 to 3:00 Break
3:00 to 3:15 Accounts payable
3:15 to 4:00 Accounts payable report
4:00 to 5:00 External interfaces

Susan: "Thank you all for meeting with me in the last few weeks. I think that I have most of the draft requirements complete. I'll read each section, and then everyone can offer comments as needed. I've obtained a sign-off from the owner of the section, but we want to make sure we aren't missing something. Does that sound good to everyone?"

They all agree.

Susan: "Ok, let's review the ordering requirements."

She reads the section. There is a 5-minute discussion. She adds in the new requirements, which are discussed as they are stated. As each new is offered, she stops the group.

Susan: "Ok Team. I just heard you propose that you wanted to auto populate the address. Does everyone agree with that?"

Everyone nods,

Susan: "Ok, good. Continue."

They discuss and add a few more lines.

Susan: "Ok, it's now time to move to Billing.

Tom: "Billing reminds me of the time I went fishing with my uncle in North Carolina...."

Susan: "Sorry, Tom. Can you tell us the story during our break at 10:00 or at lunch time? We have lots of breaks in the schedule, so you can tell us during one of them."

Tom: "Sure!"

She continues reviewing the items and moving thru the agenda on time.

Susan: "Now we need to talk about credit check."

Sarah: "I am worried about our credit checking service. I think its not working. I put my cousin in there, and she passed, and I know that's wrong."

Susan: "That's a good point. I am going to add that to the parking lot. Let's set up a meeting next week to do a deep dive into it."

Sarah: "Thanks Susan!"

Sarah continued to stay on schedule, and even finished a little early. Because of the breaks, everyone stayed fresh and sharp. They didn't get sluggish as the day went on. They felt motivated because they could see their leaders were organized and paying attention. They didn't need to repeat things.

Let's review the things that Susan did well:

1. She published the agenda before the meeting.
2. She showed up early.
3. She was realistic, giving one break every hour.
4. She stopped irrelevant topics from being discussed.
5. She put items into the parking lot that require their own meeting.
6. She drafted requirements already gathered that she could just review with the team.
7. She documented requirements as they were mentioned, and then asked everyone to verify her notes.

Discipline means that each person is focused on the meeting. At the bare minimum, the participants are not distracted by their email, playing with their cell phones, having side conversations. Either you must set the ground rules upfront, or you must deal with repeating things over and over. This wastes lots of time. When you think about how much money the company is spending on a meeting, having any of the time wasted on repetition is just unacceptable. If you set an expectation that everyone will focus for a few hours, and get a lot accomplished up front, then group pressure will forestall violations of the accepted code of conduct. The shame brought to the few violators will bring them around to walk the line. Practice setting guidelines in smaller meetings so that your team will get used to them when the time comes for the big meeting.

Time consciousness will allow you to cover all the items on your agenda. To do this, create your agenda with your realistic times. Then when you start a section, say out loud as a reminder that "We have 30 minutes to discuss storing the customer's information," for instance. Halfway thru the discussion, make a comment that "It's been 15 minutes," then another one when "We have 10 minutes left," and then for 5 minutes. This keeps everyone on track. Any task stretches to meet the time allotted for it. When you keep timelines tight, you force people to be disciplined in their thoughts, and you can get more done. If you create a sense of urgency, people will respond and come up with solutions much easier.

Clarity enables the requirements to be easily read later by a variety of stakeholders with understanding. The best way to accomplish clarity is to document each requirement in a full sentence, and ensure that all acronyms are defined. Then have the requirement read aloud for the entire team. Ask if there are any questions before moving on. Reread the sentence with the mind of a team member who isn't there. Does the requirement have enough information to be clear if you weren't there for the discussion? If not, make sure any missing words are added. Don't allow unclear requirements to be left in the document.

What do you do when you can't resolve an issue, and it's taking up time? If issues are raised that go back and forth, you need to classify the issue, get consensus, and then take the right actions. Let's look at some classifications:

Issue:
There is a missing person who knows or has an opinion on the requirement.
Resolution:
Table the topic until the person can attend and give the information or opinion.
Preemptive:
When you review the agenda, and you identify subjects that the subject matter expert can't attend the main requirements meeting, hold a private meeting with the expert to make a decision on that subject.
Issue:
There is an unknown that no individual person can be identified to answer.

Resolution:

Table the topic, and schedule a "deep dive" meeting with the subject matter experts to make a best guess.

Preemptive:

When you review the agenda and you identify subjects that are without a subject matter expert, hold a meeting with the closest expert to make a decision on the direction.

Issue:

Strong disagreement between stakeholders on a requirement.

Resolution:

Table the topic, and schedule a "deep dive" meeting between the stakeholders. Have the stakeholders each bring a summary, pros and cons of their point of view. Have each side review their supporting materials. If they can't decide based on their own discussion, escalate to their management to make the decision.

Preemptive:

When you review the agenda, and you identify hot topics, try to talk to the parties beforehand to work out any potential conflicts.

Issue:

People continually bring up subjects not currently being discussed

Resolution:

Create a list in plain sight of everyone called "The Parking Lot." Whenever an off-topic yet important subject comes up, add it to the list. Then either schedule another meeting, or add it to the end of the agenda, if there is time.

Preemptive:

Set up ground rules that attendees can just ask that any pertinent subject be added to the parking lot, without starting to discuss it at that time.

Issue:

A requirement can't be written without a decision that can't be made right now, for any of the reasons above.

Resolution:

Table it until the issue is resolved. Move to the next requirement or section.

Preemptive:

Review your agenda and think of prerequisites. If you identify an issue that needs to be resolved before a requirement can be established, set up a meeting before the requirements session to resolve it.

Now let's move to the definition of "attributes driven requirements." Every system has attributes driven requirements that are either stated or encapsulated in the minds of the clients. In their important book, *Software Architecture in Practice* by Len Bass, Paul Clements and Rick Kazman, they list the key quality attributes that clients often overlook but need to be documented.

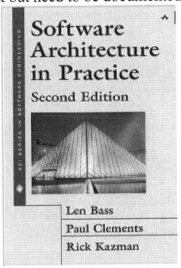

Figure 6: Cover of Software Architecture in Practice by Len Bass, Paul Clements, Rick Kazman

Let's look at a few of them
Availability
Modifiability
Security
Testability
Usability
Check out their book to get more details on each.

Modeling

There are many ways to model your architecture. The three reasons we want to model our architecture follow: accurate representation of processes, ability to run simulations under different scenarios, and ability to optimize the process.

You need to create the right documentation that your team and your stakeholders need. You might have to create several of these types of documentation. Each different stakeholder will have different requirements. Let's look at the different stakeholders, and what they likely require.

Developers

Use cases, interface specs and flow charts will all help the developer whose main goal is to write code that works.

Managers/Leads

Flow charts and end-to-end system diagrams will help the manager and lead because they want to know the bigger picture.

Project Manager

End-to-end system diagrams will help the project manager understand how all the systems interface.

Testers

Use cases, interface specs, system flow charts and end-to-end system diagrams will help the tester write their test cases.

Upper Management and Clients

An abstract view of the system and end-to-end system diagram will help upper management to understand what they are spending money on.

Users

Use cases and an abstract view of the system will help the user to understand the way they can use the system.

I'll review a few modeling techniques, but the most popular and useful models are diagramic, meaning picture-based, and textual. Let's look at where we use each of these.

Here's some of the modeling that is out there.

* Diagrammatic models - Simple and communicative
* Formal/mathematical models - Consistent but complex
* Business process languages - New and executable

Today's Modeling Techniques include:

* Flow charts- Diagrammatic models
* IDEF- Diagrammatic models

* RAD - Diagrammatic models
* UML - Diagrammatic models/ business process languages
* Petri-nets - Diagrammatic models/ Formal/mathematical models
* Business process models based on mathematical or algorithmic models- Formal/mathematical models
* BPEL/BPML- Business process languages
* jPDL- Diagrammatic models /Business process languages

Let's look at an example in several of the techniques on the "Provisioning Use Case"

First check out a textual version of the system:

1. Order Entry system must Validate the customer's address.
2. Order Entry system must Retrieve a Telephone number from Backend system.
3. Order Entry system must Negotiate product.
4. Order Entry system must Negotiate features.
5. Order Entry system must Gather customer information.
6. Order Entry system must Submit order to Backend system.
7. Backend system must Validate order information.
8. Backend system must Assign switch.
9. Backend system must Update TN status.
10. Backend system must Hold order for dispatch.
11. Backend system must Dispatch order to tech.
12. Backend system must Receive confirmation of dispatch work complete.
13. Backend system must Activate TN on switch.
14. Backend system must Send 'provisioning complete' message to billing system with order.
15. Billing system must Update billing information.
16. Billing system must Send letter to customer with account information.
17. Billing system must Send first bill.

Diagrammatic

A picture is worth a thousand words in architecture.

Diagrammatic models are pictorial diagrams of a system, usually using blocks and arrows to describe how data flows thru a system. The graphics show a simplistic view of the system without details of the process steps. Non-technical people can quickly view a diagrammatic model to understand the system represented.

There are many different versions and standards in the industry, which fall under this category: Flowcharts, IDEF, and Petri-nets.

UML Visual Use Case

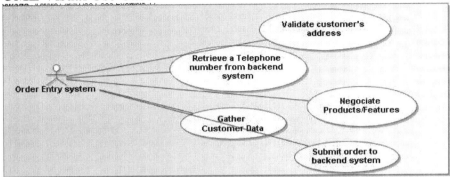

Figure 7: UML Visual Use Case

You can understand the process flow quickly just from quickly glancing at the image. A UML activity flow chart is employed below:

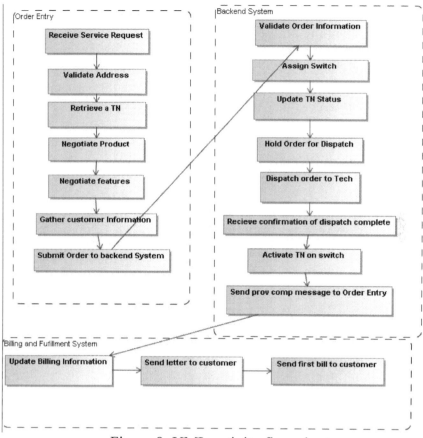

Figure 8: UML activity flow chart

IDEF Flow Chart

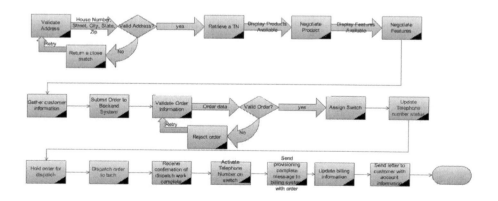

Figure 9: IDEF Flow Chart

"IDEF" initially stood for "ICAM DEFinition" language; the IEEE standards recast IDEF as "Integration DEFinition."

There are several flaws with diagrammatical models. They lack formal semantics, which means anyone can create whatever they want. There are few standards which are widely accepted. They also lack quantitative information. There is no formal underpinning to ensure consistency. Also, interpretation is expert–dependant, so it's like being at art class again, trying to determine what the artist might have meant.

The pros of diagrammatical models are that they are a way to describe the system quickly to someone at a high level. I think all systems should have some diagrammatical model's, along with other documentation.

Formal/mathematical models

The Pros:

Formal/mathematical models on the other hand contain the formal semantics. They are rigorous and precise. We can use mathematics to analyze them, and verify they are consistent. There is little ambiguity in their interpretation.

The Cons:

There is a lack of formal methods to support the design of processes.

a. Most business process elements and constraints are of a qualitative nature.
b. Business processes are hard to characterize in a formal, analytical way.
c. Representing a system is very complicated.
d. No representation for decision points, feedback loops, and parallel or hierarchical flows.
e. Difficult to maintain and retain is consistency.

Business process languages

Business process languages are the most recent generation of business process modeling methods. They are usually XML-based and use similar software development techniques. The biggest advantage is that you can actually execute them and simulate the system.

Flow charts

Flow charts fall under the category of Diagrammatic models

The only way to really simulate a business process is in a test environment that is a duplicate of the production environment. When the systems involve human actions, they become even more complicated to simulate. As a system architect, I need to know if my design is going to work. But the flaws in my designs aren't usually the kind you can pick out by looking at a graphical diagram of my process. Also the systems I design aren't fuzzy. They have specific rules for how to route an order.

Where things get fuzzy is in flushing out all the transition rules. There is a large amount of data sent on each order. Each step looks at different parts of the order to determine which next step to take. There is a transition function for each step, with hundreds of variables. To catalog each of these variables takes a large group of Subject Matter Experts from all over the company, each with expertise in different areas of the business.

The development of a large business process involved many steps, one of which is the architecture of the process. If it's a large business, then the entry point may be geographically spread out. This means that your entry points need to converge at some point if you have limited resources to share. Geographic distribution means that decisions need to be made about where physically to anchor certain steps. Once a system becomes geographically distributed, it must rely on network connects to transport data from one step to the next. These connections bring uncertainty into the system. Network connections can go down or become congested, leading to lost messages. A very reliable queuing system needs to be put in place to ensure messages are received.

Each step in the process is not just made up of substeps, but rather is also made up of several other pieces not easily modeled, each with their own issues. The following is a list of the pieces and their related issues.

1. Database
   a. Sharing data across distributed systems
2. Network
   a. Slow/unreliable connections
   b. Firewall issues
   c. Queuing systems

3. Hardware
    a. Physical redundancy
    b. Resource limitations
    c. Backups
    d. Breakdowns
4. Actual code
    a. Previous logic encoded into the software
    b. Memory leaks and other code issues
    c. Flaws of the language
5. Operating system
    a. Security holes
    b. Management of resources
6. Developers
    a. Not understand the requirements fully
    b. Create errors
    c. Not understand the best practices of coding
7. Users
    a. Do unexpected things to break the system
    b. Need training on every change
    c. Not best practices when using the system
8. Project Managers/Architects/SMEs
    a. May not be able to communicate due to difference in background.
    b. Ambiguous language may not be detected until the project is complete and   malfunction occurs.
    c. May have different agendas

In conclusion, documentation of your system's architecture is crucial. You need to create the documentation that your team needs to be able to create the system, and to allow your system to be modified and used long after you are not involved.

Soft Skills: Communication

You should have been there when I was 16 years old climbing to the third floor of the Bed and Breakfast I worked at in Key West Florida. I had spent the previous evening reading a book called "Personal Communication." I was working with my boss, the owner of the B&B, and I mentioned to her the book. "So I've been reading a book on personal communication." My boss responded, "Personal communications sounds interesting." I responded, "Yes, it doesn't matter what I know; if I can't communicate it, then it's useless."

As I've grown, that statement has become more and more true. I've watched careers of those around me dwindle and die due to lack of communication skills. Most IT people believe they can get by with their superior technical skills. They think that if they can optimize the database or keep the web server running, or bang out a new app, they won't need to write a document, talk with clients, or give a presentation to their directors.

This lack of comprehension on how the work place actually works would be funny if it wasn't so terribly sad. Getting the code complete, the web server running, and the database optimized is a very important part of the job, but we often need those folks to describe their plan for optimization to upper management, or even to the rest of the team. No one works in a vacuum. All IT work is done in teams now. It's not good enough to do the actual IT work; you need to write a plan for what you need to do, document the design at several different levels for different audiences, including your peers, your management, your upper management and clients. The more crucial the IT task you are performing, the more critical it is that everyone feels comfortable with the solution. The reason why is that today everything is a about repeatable processes. Figure something out once, document it, and then hire the lowest paid person who can perform the task to do it. Companies want to keep their key IT team working on the problems without simple solutions that may have already been found. IT is a problem-solving cost center. IT must identify problems, identify solutions, document, explain, then automate or at least make a repeatable process to run the solution. The days of hacking code out on your own are over. So what are the communication skills that you need to be a valued member of your team, and how do you get them?

They are interpersonal communication, writing and public speaking. Entire libraries are written on interpersonal communication skills, so I'll just go over a few rules of thumb that I use, and have found to be very helpful.

The first thing an architect can use is the 'mirroring effect.' People will treat you as you've treated them. If they come to you angry, and you treat them with patience and kindness, they will most likely change their attitude. Always treat people respectfully, and they will most likely do the same to you. If you can do something nice for them, they will be more likely to say yes when you need something from them.

Listening is a discipline that takes time to develop and become competent. It's a constant effort, but it's the fundamental skill of communication. I am often sent into failing projects. I arrive and listen. I interview each key person and ask open ended questions and listen very carefully to their words. I write down what they say. After only a few days, I can usually figure out from where the problems are stemming. Listening is the number one skill I use to be successful at my job. I see its importance each day. People who are powerful listeners outperform those who are distracted listeners. Those who don't focus and listen never have an advantage over those who have listened powerfully. The advantage is that the powerful listener knows so much more, and knowledge is power. They can use all the tiny facts they gleaned just from listening to make better decisions, predict problems and avoid them.

So how does one actually listen? Let's look at an example illustrating how you can best get needed information from a colleague or your boss. First, document a few questions that you need answered before you go into the conversation. Then initiate the conversation without distractions, meaning put down the cell phone, ignore or turn off your instant messenger, turn off or ignore your email, close your sports update browser and don't think about lunch. Just focus your attention on the speaker. Listen to each word, and don't think about what you are going to say in response. Instead let them talk as much as they need to; then when they stop, ask them a question about what you just heard or one you had previously written. Take notes. Taking notes works for you in three ways. First it shows the person you are talking with that you respect their time and their information so much that you are writing it down. Second, it helps you to affix what they are saying in your mind so that you'll really remember it. And third, it allows you to reference these notes later instead of bothering them again about the same issue.

At the end of a conversation, recap all the important points and any action items that were mentioned. Ask for agreement on the important points and action items before leaving the conversation.

When you are listening, it's more than just hearing the words. You should also maintain eye contact, listen for the tone of voice and watch the body language. If someone can't make eye contact with you while you are having a conversation, you will never trust that person. You must make sure that eye contact is maintained without staring.

Tone of voice is also important to observe. Is your boss upset about something? If she sounds angry, then ask if anything else is going on. Often on a call someone will answer a question in a tone of boredom. This will be a cue to me that they aren't really listening. They might not have heard the question completely, and need to listen to it again so that you can be sure their answer is correct. As the architect, you are on constant alert of subtext. You need to look for issues that haven't risen to the surface yet. You need to find those subtexts and dig in because that's where the issues lie that might destroy your project.

Observing body language is another important part of listening. Many times someone will be saying one thing with their voice, but their body is telling another story. If they tell you that it's no problem to write that interface, but they are hunched over and cowering, you might want to ask if there's any issues they can foresee. Very likely there's some problem that you need to uncover.

If you can always listen powerfully, then you'll have an advantage over most other IT people. So make sure you master listening.

In the book *So What's your Point?* by James C. Wetherbe and Bond Wetherbe, they give models for verbal communication. I highly recommend you read it. Here are the highlights. The models at a high level are as follows:

1. **Explanation Model-** Used when you are explaining something to someone. You need to first give the problem, and then give the solution. It's important not to swap these two.

2. **Agreement Model** – Used after you have explained, and now the person you are communicating with agrees with you. You need to reinforce the agreement by saying "you're right" or something similar, and expand on why they are right to agree with you.

3. **Closure Model** – Used after you've communicated the points you wanted to make, and obtained agreement. Closure Model consists of reviewing the points, followed by a proposed course of action.

4. **Reservation/Doubt Model**- Used when the person you are communicating with doesn't believe either the problem you've stated is a real problem or that the solution you gave will work. At this point you don't want to get emotional. First you need to reassure the person their reservation or doubt is something you also care about. Then you need to substantiate the problem by reiterating, but making sure to elaborate on the reasons why it's a real problem.

5. **Question/Confusion/Conflict Model** – Used when the person you are communicating with has questions, confusion or conflict. First rephrase the person's question with, "You are concerned with, <issue>?" Make sure you say it in a way that is respectful. Get to the heart of the issue. If they say, "No I am concerned with something else," then rephrase that concern. Make sure you really understand their concern clearly. Once they agree that you have rephrased their question correctly, and then you can answer, clarify or minimize that concern exactly. When you minimize their concern, you do it by reviewing the alternatives to the use of your solution. Show that your solution outweighs the cost of not doing your solution.

6. **Query Model** - Used if the person you are communicating with just says "No" to your request without any information; then you need to use the query model. An indirect probe is saying, "Oh?" If they still just say "No" without giving any more information, then you should start guessing what their concern might be.

Stay respectful at every stage of these interactions. Let's look at some role playing with two of our architects. The situation is that the system being developed needs new hardware. The architect wants their director to approve the request.

Now let's look at a bad example of the conversation for this situation.

John: "Hi Ralph. I came to talk about the hardware that you said you'd meet me about."

Ralph: "Yes come in and sit."

John: "Ralph, [**Solution**] we need to buy a more powerful server, as I've laid out in the email I sent you.

Ralph: [**Doubt of the problem**] "We just bought that hardware two years ago. I don't want to buy hardware that we don't need."

John:[**offended**] "You think I didn't check if we really need the hardware?"

Ralph: "Well, I don't understand why we need more."

John: "If we don't get it, the new system won't work."

Ralph: [**Conflict**] "We don't have any budget for new hardware."

John: [**Offended**] "You only care about the budget?"

Ralph: "Yes, that's right; I don't think our upper management will approve that extra expense."

John: "Our upper management never understands what we are trying to do."

Ralph: "Right."

John: "This project is going to fail. I tried to save it."

Ralph: "Hmm. I do not understand why you need new hardware, John."

John: [**Explain the problem**] "The hardware isn't fast enough to support the new demand of our customer service reps."

Ralph: "Oh. I didn't realize that. Did you really try to get the hardware to work?"

John: [**Offended**] "Of course."

Ralph: "Well I am not sure we have the budget."

John: "Oh well. You'll see when we launch, and it doesn't work."

Ralph: "Why don't you come back when you have some proof."

John: "Whatever!"

Now let's look at the same situation with someone using the correct models:

Susan: "Hi Ralph. [**Verify this is a good time and they are not being distracted by something else**] Is this still a good time to discuss the hardware for the new system?"

Ralph: "Yes, come in and sit."

Susan: "Ralph, [**Explain the problem**] the new system will be used by all 500 of our customer service representatives constantly throughout the day. To meet our aggressive goals of response time to our customers, we need to have a system that exceeds our current hardware limitations. The director of the customer service representatives has clearly given us response-time requirements. We have tested the current hardware with the new software, and it is not meeting those response times.

[**Give the solution**] To handle that type of traffic, we need to buy a more powerful server, as I've laid out in the email I sent you."

Ralph: [**Doubt of the problem**] "We just bought that hardware two years ago. I don't want to buy hardware that we don't need."

Susan:[**Reassure**] "We certainly don't want to buy hardware we don't need."

Ralph: "Exactly."

Susan: [**Substantiate**] "Here is what we are up against. We have robust software that will be collecting a lot more data, and responding a lot quicker to customer service representatives than our current software. We just can't handle that type of transaction within the requested response time using our current hardware. Our best techs have tested it with a variety of configurations. It's taking well over the acceptable limits to meet our requirements."

Ralph: [**Conflict**] "We don't have any budget for hardware."

Susan: [**Rephrase with a validation of the communication**] "Let me make sure I understand, you are concerned with the budget for hardware?"

Ralph: "Yes, that's right; I don't think our upper management will approve that extra expense."

Susan: [**Rephrase again with a validation of the communication**] "Ok, so you are worried that we won't get approval from upper management?"

Ralph: "Right."

Susan: [**Minimize**] "So the alternative is that we deliver a system that doesn't allow our company to meet its response-time goals. That will stop us from winning the best customer service award we are applying for. If you are worried about getting approval, I can put the business case together for upper management so that they will understand the issue and what is at stake."

Ralph: "Hmm. My end of year is based on us getting that award for customer service."

Susan: [**Reinforce**] "Good point!

[**Expand**] If we don't get the faster server, we won't be able to win that award, and that award will really get us a lot of press coverage and put us ahead of our competition.

Ralph: [**Agreement**] "That's so true."

Susan: [**Points of agreement**] "So to get this hardware to ensure we meet our response- time goals, [**Propose course of action**] you can click 'accept' on the hardware ordering site, and I'll send over the documentation to review the business case."

Ralph: "Ok, I'll approve it, and if they ask, then we can send them your documentation. Thanks for being so thorough in this, Susan."

Susan: "Glad to do it Ralph. Thanks for the time, and have a great afternoon."

As we saw in this dialog, the model works very well. Read the full book to learn the way to handle difficult people.

Listening carefully can get you a long way in architecture. Listening is the main interpersonal communication skill you need. When you respond with an attitude of respect for the relationship you have with the person you're communicating with, your conversations will be effective. Make sure your main goal in each conversation is furthering trust. I have often found myself working with people over and over with different hierarchal relationships. So your 'direct report' now, might be your boss later, so watch out how you talk to each person. Make sure it's always respectful. You must not create enemies as an architect. It will severely damage your ability to be effective.

Writing skills are also necessary as an architect for two main reasons. First, you will be writing documentation. If you write clear and concise documents, they will save you from having to clarify and answer questions later. Second, you'll be writing a lot of email. The better you can respond to a question via email, the more effectively you can avoid a meeting or a follow-up call.

Your writing in documentation and emails needs to be grammatically correct. I once received an email from a manager that went something like the following:

i think the file cud b sent over ftp. ill let u know soon.
tnx

I immediately called him and asked if he thought that this email was an excellent representation of what a manager should write. He thought about it for a while, and then told me he thought that I was correct, and that he would start mending his ways. Your email is just as important as your documentation. Make sure you sound professional and respectful in it. Often, email is sequestered as part of audits. Don't write things in it that are inappropriate. It's very embarrassing to you and your company. Read *The Elements of Style* by William Strunk Jr., E. B. White to get a good summary of writing guidelines.

Public speaking is another communication skill that you must master to be a successful software architect. As often quoted, most people are more afraid of public speaking than they are of death. If you can master giving a memorable and persuasive speech, you will be unstoppable as an architect. Quite often you will need to convince a group of people that your viewpoint on a design or technology is superior. Let's look at two different openings, and then examine what worked and what didn't work. The situation is that two architects, John and Susan, each have a different solution for a search engine:

John comes into the room wearing jeans and an un-tucked t-shirt bearing the logo, "My dog is better than your honor student." During his presentation, he never looked at the audience; instead he read off his slide. His slides were big blocks of very small text.

"Hi everyone. I am sorry about the presentation I am about to give. I haven't gotten much sleep lately, and I didn't get a chance to do a lot of research. I kinda threw some points together so I hope you won't mind.

So a search engine should be fast. This technology is really hot right now. Let's look at it….."

After John's presentation, Susan stands up, and she is wearing a suit. She looked her audience in the eyes throughout the speech. Her slides were clear, with very few points on each. She used graphics to illustrate her points.

"In order to serve our customers, our customer service team must get to their data faster than our competition. We must provide excellent customer service or we all will be searching for a new job. That's why I am asking you to consider the amazing benefits of this technology for search….

Now the technologies themselves may have been equal or maybe John's was better. But guess who is going to be taken more seriously as an expert on the subject. Giving an excellent presentation is just as important as being an expert on the technology, if not more important.

I'll review some tools that will help you to give a great presentation. Using these tools of public speaking effectively is the difference between getting your design accepted, as opposed to being flat-out rejected. Make sure you prepare for your speech. The more preparation you do, the more confident you will be for your speech.

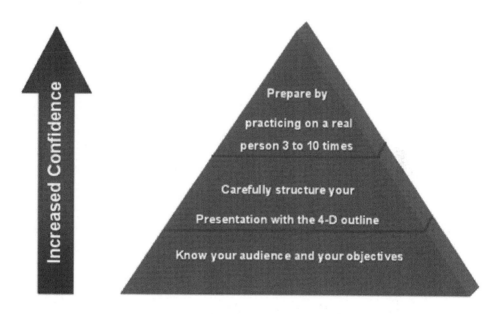

Figure 10: Public Speaking Chart

First, know your audience. What is their level of expertise? What are they expecting? What is their attitude going in? Know if they are executives or developers, project managers or trainers. Each of these groups will have different expectations for your presentation. Do your research well in advance of your presentation. Ask those who know about the audience.

Second, know your objective. Why are you giving this presentation? What do you hope to accomplish? What do you want your audience to do next? If you are giving your presentation to an executive, then you need to propose a clear outline of the steps you want him or her to take after your presentation.

Third, you need to use the '4-D outline.' This is a technique I adapted from Tony Jeary's book, *Life is a Series of Presentations*. You must read his book. The 4-D outline allows you to structure your speech in a way that meets your objectives powerfully within your time limits. The format will be as follows.

* Time for each point.
* What each point is.
* Why covering that point is important.
* How you want to make that point.

For example
Time: From 11:00 to 11:05
What: Welcome everyone and explain today's agenda.
Why: To allow everyone to feel comfortable and understand what we are covering.
How: Verbally welcome and hand out a printed agenda.

Time	What	Why	How
11:00 to 11:02	Welcome everyone and explain today's agenda.	To allow everyone to feel comfortable and understand what we are covering.	Verbally welcome and hand out a printed agenda.

Figure 11: 4D outline

Then prepare the rest of your points following this technique. To continue the example:
Time: from 11:05-11:15
What: Review System Architecture.
Why: To get buy-in from the Director on the architecture so that we can move forward.
How: Insert into the PowerPoint the end-to-end architecture graphics 1 and 2. Walk the audience through each step of the flow.

ime	What	Why	How
1:05-11:15	Review System Architecture.	To get buy in from the Director on the architecture so that we can move forward.	Insert into the PPT the end -to-end architecture graphics 1 and 2. Walk the audience through each step of the flow.

Figure 12: 4D Outline Example

Fourth, design a spectacular opening. Never start with an apology about anything. Your audience might have been in several meetings before yours, or even in several presentations before yours. You need to wake them up with energy. Tell them why this is so important to them right now. Make them recognize the need to pay attention.

Fifth, focus on a clear presentation body. Keep your body to 3 points. Don't overwhelm your audience. Tell a story to illustrate any points (if you can). Look at your audience while you are speaking. Practice in front of a mirror to check your body language. You need to stand straight and tall, without fidgeting. Be energetic! Do NOT be Monotone! Use pauses for emphases. Vary your voice's speed.

Keep your slides simple. Use graphics when you can. Here are some examples of bad slides:

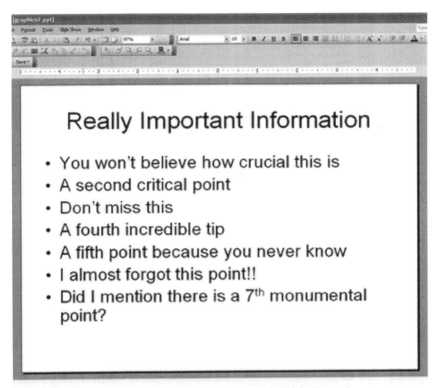

Figure 13: Example of a Bad Slide Part 1

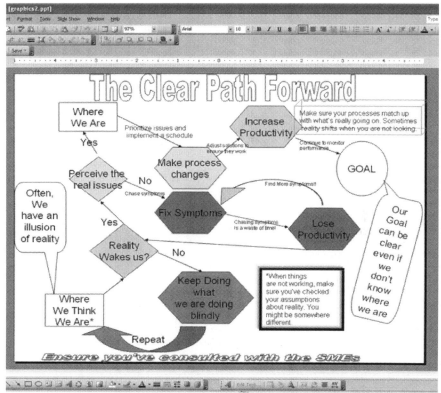

Figure 14: Example of a Bad Slide Part 2

Sixth, wrap it up with style. Be sure to summarize important points. Make sure you have the next steps listed. Ensure your call to action is very clear. Mention any risks involved if your plan is not executed in a timely manner. People are always motivated more strongly by what they are going to lose, rather than by what they will gain.

If you start adding these communication skills into your daily work as an IT professional, no matter what you are doing, you will have a completive advantage over your colleagues, and move ahead much faster.

Soft Skills: Negotiation/Consensus Building

Life is a series of negotiations, and that is even truer as an architect. There are many great books on negotiation. One such is *Getting to Yes* by Roger Fisher.

You should have listened in on my negotiation with the owner of a system that we needed to integrate into our main architecture. His system provided some accounts payable services that we required. His negotiation stand was to control much of the system's end-to-end flow. My view as the architect was that his system should control a very small part, just around the accounts payable function. The main thing to remember when negotiating with another system owner is that their ego is tied up in their system's prestige. They want to feel important. I had to be very careful as I talked with him, so that he didn't feel like his system was being giving a less important role in the overall architecture. Never demean or belittle anyone.

Every interaction should be aimed at building trust. He had been arguing for at least three years with the architecture team about the role of his application. I had only recently joined the project, so I hadn't experienced the history first hand. I realized that I had a huge mountain to cross to get to a compromise. I spent the first few hours reviewing their architectural proposal with an open mind. One thing the owner said over and over was that his team had won many awards. He said he had a whole bunch of them on his desk because his system was so excellent. I really paid attention to what they actually were asking for.

After listening a lot and asking questions on their system to show that I was paying attention, I told them about the role that we would like them to play. I told him the following, "If we can get this project completed on schedule, then we will all receive awards for it. Your architecture isn't far from what we were envisioning. What if I make a few adjustments and send it over."
He said, "Ok I'll look at it"
I sent over the slight adjustments, keeping as much as I could the same.
When we met again, he and his team accepted my modifications.
The main things that I did were:
1. Keep an open mind.
2. Be respectful, with a goal of building trust.

3. Listen carefully for what they actually wanted, and for common ground.
4. Know the absolute core of what you require.
5. Use what you learn to craft a compromise suited to both sides.

My teammates were in shock when I let them know about the compromise. Often, teams will not listen to each other, so if you come in and actually listen, you will be a highly valuable member of the team.

Consensus building is a milder form of negotiations, but used more inside the team itself. You need to build consensus when team members have opinions on the architecture that are in conflict with other members. There're a few techniques to really help you in this situation.

First, have the members clearly document their solution with pros and cons. Second, review the assumptions and proposals with the whole team. . Once all the vetting questions have been asked, ask the team which solution best fits. Most of the time, some compromise can be generated. Often, team members have not thought their ideas through, so even putting together the documentation on their solution will open their eyes to the problems in their solution.

When you are creating an architecture with the team, make sure that each section is agreed upon. This will limit the number of complaints later.

Sometimes people think that when they become an architect, they can dictate whatever solution they dream up, without the consensus of the team. But that is very wrong.

Building consensus allows you to be sure your architecture will be implemented. As architects, we can only design and hand over the design to the development team. We have no control to actually implement the design. Thus our power lies only in achieving agreement to the architecture.

Soft Skills: Project Manager and the Architect Relationship

I've been both a project manager and an architect, so I can confidently speak on both of these subjects. The relationship between the two is a partnership. The architect must be the partner of the IT project manager; together as a team, they make the project a success. Let's explore some of their joint responsibilities.

The architect serves as a spokesperson for the project architecture. When any stakeholders such as developers, testers, clients, users or executives want to see what the architecture is, the architect needs to develop a view of the system to suit the audience, and review it with them. The architect needs to be able to explain any aspect of the systems function. The project manager should be able to ask the architect about impacts to other external systems, and the architect should then do the research, and give a timely response.

The PM's role is to manage the project, and coordinate the project. Timelines, project plans, work breakdown structures, work assignments, cost management and procurements are all responsibilities of the project manager.

The architect plus the PM are the face of IT to the clients. The architect needs to be a trustworthy person whom the clients really rely on to give them the facts straight. Clients and users are often worried about changes to their system, which they rely on for their livelihood. They want to be confident that IT knows what it's doing. Since clients don't usually have access to the developer writing the code, the only people by which they can judge all of IT by is by the PM and the architect. The architect has the authority to speak on the functionality of the system, and must give the stakeholders confidence. You must be a walking personification of IT and the system.

The architect is the cross-functional design leader for the project, providing insight into technical, business and operational aspects. The architect must be ready to give overviews on any of these areas of the project, tailored to the requesting audience. These presentations should imbibe the audience with confidence.

The architect displays the importance of the project, and helps drive project team members towards an objective common solution. The attitude of the architect is reflected by each member of the team. Attitudes are very contagious. If the architect behaves as though the project doesn't really matter, or that it won't be successful, then the team members will start adopting this attitude. The energy the architect brings to the project is infectious to the entire project staff. It's important to believe in the project, and want to do an excellent job. At each meeting, make sure you are pumped up and excited. Explain the importance of the project regularly to ensure everyone is on the same page. If you have quotes from stake holders on how important the project is, make sure you share them with the team. This energy is the difference between a project that falls behind and one that says on schedule.

The architect plus the PM must consider the success of the project their personal responsibility. If the architect doesn't think that they have any influence on the project, then they will act that way and that will interfere with whole project. The architect is very important to the success of the project and recognizing that fact will go a long way to ensuring the project's success.

Soft Skills: Time Management

The skill that will determine if you become an architect at all, or if you are one already, whether you are effective at time management. Let's look at John and Susan to see which one will be the effective architect.

It's 9:00 am on Monday when John sits down at his computer. He immediately goes to his email, and starts perusing through the 50 new messages. After reviewing 20 of them, all of which need some response, he instead answers those few that are easiest to dispense. Then his calendar application issues a a 15-minute alert for his upcoming 10:00 am review of the new architecture with the team. He realizes that he should have finalized a few interfaces before the call. He quickly looks on the company instant-messenger buddy list for the contacts for those systems, finds two contacts, and IM's them. He asks them his questions, and they respond just barely in the nick of time. He starts to update the diagram with needed information, but then Bob stops by his cube. He's got 5 minutes before his review.

Bob says, "Hi John, you didn't tell me if I can use your address validation service, and I need to give a presentation in 5 minutes."

John realizes that he was supposed to do that research this morning to verify that he had all the data points that Bob needed. Bob had asked him to do so on Friday afternoon. John says, "Oh man. I am so sorry, dude. I'll have to check after my 10:00 am meeting."

Bob says, "John, these guys only had this time slot this week. Now my deadline is going to have to be pushed out by a week."

John says, "I am sorry man!"

John finally dials into the phone conference 5 minutes late, after he finishes updating his diagram. Everyone is really irritated because he is late again.

John says, "Sorry guys, I had to finish one last thing in my design. But you're going to really love it."

Judy on the call says, "John, we already started reviewing my diagram that I put together. I think that we will probably just go with my architecture for this project since you seem to not have it together."

When John gets off the call he is very disappointed, so he decides to check out the scores for his favorite team. He gets into reading an article all about the game over the weekend, and forgets about time.

His phone rings at 11:30, "John, this is Tom. I found a problem with the system you architected last month."

Tom is a user. John knows that Tom is a user who talks for a long time.

John says, "OK Tom. What did you find?"

Tom goes on and on about how the system was suppose to be so user friendly, but he already found a bug after only a few weeks, and he is really tired of getting systems that aren't fully tested. Finally, he tells John the actual issue. "Well, I was doing my end of the month reports, and I noticed that when I clicked the 'export as Excel' it actually gave me a .csv file instead of an Excel file."

John says, "Just open Excel, and then use the 'file open' box to open the .csv. That type of file opens in Excel."

After a moment of silence, Tom says, "Oh, OK. Thanks."

John's calendar pops up with another 15-minute alert for a noon call with his director to review two alternative approaches to a storage issue. He realizes he forgot to put the presentation together. He starts working on it right away, but he never finishes, and shows up to the meeting with very poor slides. After the meeting, which John's manager attended, his manager asks him to walk to his office.

Seated across from his manager, Larry says, "John, we gave you the architecture position because you are a highly creative developer. You always impress us with your novel ideas, but it seems that you are always unprepared for meetings and presentations. We are going to return you to developer status for now, until you develop better time-management skills."
John walked back to his cube dejected, wondering what went wrong, but then he decides not to worry about it, and get something to eat.

Now let's look at Susan with the same schedule and requirements.
Susan sits down at her desk at 9:00 am on Monday. She does not open her email. She first opens her calendar to see if anyone added any more meetings. She sees she has a 10:00 am call, and a noon meeting with her director. She next opens her TO DO list and reviews the things she added on Friday. Her TO DO list looks like the following:
TO DO
Critical
   * Verify that address validation web service has availability for Bob's project.
   * Research Interfaces for 10 am call. Contact Sam from Billing and Linda from Shipping.
   * Create PPT for storage alternatives. Check the intranet site, which has the data needed.
Should Do
   * Respond to email about next week's conference.
   * Schedule review of the UUR proposal.
Could Do
   * Make sure Sara has the user docs completed.
   She has to finish the interfaces for the 10:00 am call, and needs to do research on the alternatives for storage for the noon meeting.
She quickly IM's Sam and Linda for the interface. They respond, and she updates the diagram. It's now 9:08 am.
She opens the web service definition, and checks if it will work for Bob. She IM's Bob, and tells him he can use the web service. He says, "Thanks! Perfect timing for my 10:00 am. The project will be on time!"
It's now 9:12 am.

She opens the intranet website, and does the research for the storage alternatives. She almost has all the information on the storage when her 5-minute alert goes off for the 10:00 am meeting. She dials into the conference, and makes sure that she is displaying her diagram before everyone else shows up. As each person dials in, she says, "Good Morning! This is Susan, who just joined?"
She starts the meeting right on time, and everyone likes her design. They finish, and she gets back to work on the storage proposal.

Her phone rings at 11:30 am, and she answers it by saying, "Good morning, this is Susan."
Tom says, "Hi this is Tom." Susan is well aware of Tom's tendency to talk a long time, and she knows she needs to finish her PowerPoint before 12:00 noon.
She responds, "Hi Tom! Great to hear from you. I have a deadline so please let me know how I can help you."
Tom says, "Well, I was doing my end-of-the-month reports, and I noticed that when I clicked the 'export as Excel,' it actually gave me a .csv file instead of an Excel file."
Susan says, "Just open Excel, and then use the 'file open' box to open the .csv. That type of file opens in Excel."
Tom is silent for a moment, and then says, "OK cool. Thanks Susan."
Susan says, "I am glad to help."

She puts the final touches on the presentation, and walks down to the meeting ten minutes early. Getting there early, she gets to chit chat with her director, Ralph. He tells her about a big project coming up, and she says she's interested in working on it. He says that he'll keep her in mind. Her manager gets there, as well as the others who need to make the decision.
She gives her presentation, which is very well put together. They are all impressed in the quality. They decide, and end the meeting early.

As she is about to leave, her manager, Fred, asks her to come to his office.
Susan, "We gave you the architecture position because you are a highly creative developer. You always impress us with your novel ideas. But now as an architect, you are really impressing us. You are always prepared. I got a call from Tom, our user, about how nice you were to him on his issue. I know it's not normal, but we have some

big projects coming down the pipeline, and you are the top of my list for designing them. Keep up the good work."

She walks back to her cube elated. When she gets back, she opens her email for the first time, and checks the subjects to see if they're about next week's conference, and responds to those first. Then she checks the other emails' subjects to decide if they are important. If one is important, she responds right away; if not, she leaves it unread so she can look at it later.

She sits back and thinks about where she wants to eat lunch. Let's look at the things that made John a poor time manager:

1. Didn't keep a TO DO list.
2. Checked his email first.
3. Didn't check his calendar.
4. Didn't respond to email, but just looked at it.
5. Didn't deal with distractive people quickly.
6. Didn't prepare for his presentations.
7. Showed up late for all his meetings, unprepared.

Let's look at the things that made Susan a good time manager.

1. She kept a prioritized TO DO list.
2. She didn't check her email first.
3. She used her calendar to keep all her meetings, and checked it often.
4. She worked on the critical items on her TO DO first.
5. She dealt with distractive people by telling them she had limited time so they would get to the point.
6. She prepared for her presentations.
7. She showed up early for meetings, prepared.

Time management is critical, as you can see. These are typical days for an architect. It's rare to not get distracted or have 50 emails. You must learn how to prioritize, and stay on top of the critical items.

Architecture Case Studies at Trim Solutions

We've looked at a variety of best practices related to software architecture. This chapter will review architecture case studies at Trim Solutions. As we go through this chapter, I'll use several real life case studies to illustrate.

Case Study One: Migration

First, let's look at a migration and decommission situation. Susan's company, Trim Solutions, an exercise equipment company, recently bought Get Slim, a small supplements company. Get Slim has several systems, including billing, inventory and customer records. Susan has been assigned as the end-to-end solutions architect for the project to migrate the Get Slim data into Trim Solution's strategic systems. The first phase of the project is to move the customer records, including the ordering system, into Trim Solution's ordering and customer records system.

First, clearly analyze the original problem. Understanding the problem is always the first step, and yet it's often forgotten. During the entire design process, think back to the original problem, and ask yourself if this new system will fix the original problem.

Susan's first thought is "What are the real problems that we are trying to fix by migrating?" One root problem is that maintaining two separate systems is expensive. The Get Slim licenses, hardware and separate team of system-support people all cost extra money. Another root problem is that Trim Solutions has one customer service center. When a customer calls about a Get Slim product, the customer service rep has to log into a separate system, and search for the customer there. This extra step increases the call volume and wait times for all customers. Trim Solutions highly values its exceptional customer service, and these wait times are driving down their rankings. Susan must therefore focus on these two root problems while designing her solution.

Second, get all the Requirements, as discussed in Chapter 14. Susan has to talk with the Get Slim system folks to understand their data. She has them walk her through the ordering screens and the customer data records screens. Then she has their architect walk her through the flowcharts for the ordering and customer records flows. She then asks to look at all outbound interfaces, reports, outbound feeds, batches and other outputs. Then she asks to look at all inbound feeds and interfaces. She observes weekly reports of orders and their statuses, and which workflow step they are in. (A workflow is a set of steps that need to be completed to finish a process.) This helps her to determine in which workflow step that orders end up in the longest, and whether there are any order statuses that she doesn't need to worry about.

Third, create the design. Susan realizes that the design in a system migration and decommission mainly focuses around data mappings. She first wants to put a design around the In Flight Orders. In Flight Orders are orders that are being processed while the system is migrated. To allow customers to receive the orders they placed for Get Slim products right before the migration, Susan needs to ensure that these orders are migrated into the Trim Solutions system, and placed into a similar order workflow step. She must first map the Get Slim order workflow steps to the Trim Solution order workflow steps.

She takes a piece of paper, and on the top half draws the Get Slim Ordering process. On the bottom half, she draws the Trim Solutions Order process. The top half has five workflow steps: validate order, accepted order, warehouse, shipped and closed.

The bottom half has six workflow steps: pre-order validation, post-order validation, accepted, warehouse, shipped and closed.

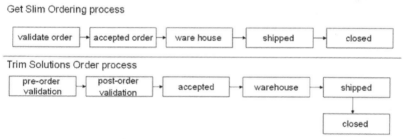

Figure 15: Get Slim Order Process

She draws lines in between the steps to show that 'pre-order validation' and 'post-order validation' map to 'validate order.' 'Accepted' maps to 'accepted order.' 'Warehouse' maps to 'warehouse.' 'Shipped' maps to 'shipped.' And 'closed' maps to 'closed.' Not too bad so far.

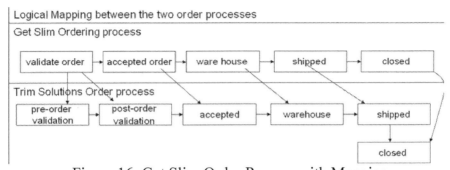

Figure 16: Get Slim Order Process with Mapping

Now she must think about exceptions. There's a few more order statuses that need to be handled: 'overdue,' 'rejected' and 'returned.' She looks at the numbers of orders in 'rejected' status, and sees that it's less than 10 at any given time. With less than 10, she will create a manual process for a user to handle the order. Often, IT folks want to write a script or program to handle everything, but really you should only automate things if it makes sense. If it takes a person 5 minutes to manually handle the issue, and there are only 10 instances of the issue ever expected, and writing a script to automate it will take a programmer 3 hours to write, a simple ROI (return on investment) calculation will show that it's more expensive to automate the process.

She looks at 'returned' status and sees its got 10k records. She calls the architect of Get Slim and asks why there's 10k.

Susan: "Joe, I am seeing 10,887 records in status of 'return.' What's the process around that?"

Joe: "We manually just credit the account when we get a product back. Those just stay like that forever."

Susan: "Can we ignore them? Or is action still required on them?"

Joe: "The problem is that we don't know which of them that manual credit has been performed on or not because there's no more granularity in the status. We'd have to go look at the account to see if a credit has been applied."

Susan: "I think we might need to create a query to check that then during the migration. If no credit has been applied, we might need to create a new workflow step in Trim Solutions."

Joe: "That's probably a good idea. There's a web service we can use to query the customer record."

Susan: "I need to go back to my clients and propose this solution to them. Thanks Joe."

Joe: "Sure thing Susan."

Susan will need to create processes around any exceptions like the 'returns' status. Once she has all the mappings laid out and processes defined for non-automated issues, she will review it with the stakeholders and make sure she hasn't missed anything.

Fourth, after the high-level processes have been mapped, she needs to do data mapping. This is where she looks at the customer records table in both Get Slim and Trim Solutions. She looks at each field and maps it to the corresponding field. New fields may need to be created in the Trim Solutions customer tables. Updates to the GUI may need to be created to allow editing of those new fields.

Fifth, she and the PM will create a detailed plan for migration with pre-migration phase, during-migration phase, and post-migration phase. The Migration plan should be minute by minute. All of this, together, needs to be represented at a high level and presented to the stakeholders for sign off.

Case Study Two: Web Portal

Now let's look at a new product that is being introduced into the Trim Solutions product line. The product is a health monitoring system. One component is a sensor chip that is worn around the customer's wrist or ankle. Other components include a scale and a refrigerator monitor camera. The chip, scale, and fridge cam send signals to the customer's iPhone via radio frequency to an iPhone attachment. The product is manufactured by a factory in South Korea. The device measures a plethora of biomedical responses. There is an iPhone app that then gives the customers graphs, and lets them keep track of their health. The web portal is uploaded with the information from the devices, and is shared with their health accountability partners. Susan is responsible for launching the web portal.

First, she needs to understand the problem. Experience has proven that individuals using the system stick to their health goals better when they share results with friends and family, or generally make it public. They also do better when they weigh themselves every day, and share that information with their accountability partners.

Second, Susan needs to gather the requirements. She creates a list of use cases. Her clients in product development give her the following list:

1. The web portal has to share the user's information only with those that the user has added to their accountability partner list.
2. User can create campaigns with health goals.
3. User can add members to their accountability partner list.
4. User can view reports from any slice of time they want from their own data.
5. User can view reports from any of their accountability partners.
6. User can send encouragement note or congratulatory note from the system.
7. User can view all the notes they receive from their accountability partners.

The list goes on, but for this example, we won't go into all the details.

Susan creates use case documents with each step defined. Let's look at one example.

Use case number seven: User can view all the notes they received.

1. User logs into the system with their login (see login use case for details).
2. User sees their home page with their 'Recently Received Notes' link.
3. User clicks on link.
4. System displays the notes with From, Subject, Type and link to read 'Full Note Text.'
5. The user clicks on the 'Full Note Text.'
6. System displays from, subject, type, and full text of note, 'Respond' button, 'Delete' button, 'Keep as New' button.
7. User clicks on 'Keep as New.'
8. System marks the read flag as 'N' in the note table.

End of Use case

Susan creates a use case for all seven items in the list from product development, and from that she can start her design.

Third, Susan creates a database layout based on the requirements; she creates mockups based on the requirements. She meets with the app server group to create an interface between their app server biometrics data and her web portal database. She gets samples of the interface definition. She studies the data, and then creates tables to store the data so that it's accessible to the web portal. Any of these steps will be actually implemented by another developer, with Susan only giving them differing levels of documentation and help, depending on their level of competency.

Fourth, she and the PM will create a detailed plan for deployment with testing and user acceptance testing. All of this needs to be represented at a high level, and presented to the stakeholders for sign-off.

Case Study Three: Interfacing with External Company

Let's look at another situation. Trim Solutions wants to give its customers a 10% discount at Total Body Fitness. Both companies plan to run a big marketing campaign as soon as the software is ready. So there's a lot of pressure from upper management to get the solution implemented. Susan must consider this as she does her design.

First, she needs to understand the opportunity. The opportunity is that customers have a 50% probability of reordering again if they feel their health solutions company has a variety of offers and extra benefits. One benefit uncovered by the market research team was that customers were interested in having discounts at a local gym. The team identified Total Body Fitness as a good cultural match, and as having locations in many of Trim Solutions' customer's areas. Susan needs to create a system to allow Total Body Fitness to identify when a client is a Trim Solutions customer, and apply the discount. Total Body Fitness will also share its customer information with Trim Solutions to allow offers to be marketed. Susan will only be working on the interface, but she needs to understand how the data will be used by the other applications to ensure that the interface meets all the requirements. The marketing team asks for weekly updates of the Total Body Fitness customer data.

Second, she interviews the Trim Solutions marketing team to understand what Total Body Fitness customer information they need in order to do their targeted marketing. She sits with them, and they tell her the input their marketing software needs. Next she interviews the IT team at Total Body Fitness to understand what their billing system needs to do to apply the discounts. The Total Body Fitness people want daily updates of customer data so they can give discounts immediately, thus avoiding disappointed customers for lack of timely system updates.. She also reviews the data she needs from their team for the marketing software. She discusses the technology choices. Owing to severe time constrictions, they jointly decide on going with **sftp** encrypted files, which will be placed on servers. Trim Solutions will place their file on their server at 12:30 am ET each day. Total Body Fitness people will place a file on their own server at 3:00 am ET every Saturday. Each partner will look for the files at the appointed time, and re-query as necessary for 3 hours before sending an email to the designated IT support group in each company.

Third, after she gets both feeds ironed out, she lays out a diagram with the different systems, and the names of the feeds between them, together with the technology used for each and the frequency of data refreshes. She reviews the architecture with the development team, testers, management and both IT teams, and makes sure everyone signs off on the design.

Fourth, she works with the PM to get the schedule completed; if necessary, she consults with anyone who has any concerns or questions.

In this case study, during the testing phase a glitch occurs. The legal team at Total Body Fitness objects to their customer data being sent to a third party. The legal team calls up Susan's director to tell him that they don't want to continue with the project. Susan's director goes to meet with the legal team's director and the Trim Solutions legal team. After several weeks of negotiating, a new contract is drawn up where only certain Total Body Fitness client information is sent, based on an opt-out flag that remained unchecked when the customer signed up. But they did agree to hang posters around the gym letting everyone know about Trim Solutions products and services, with instructions on how to get on the program with the discount.

Susan has to delay the project's code until the final go-ahead from legal is given. These kinds of delays will happen, and you will need to deal with them, and let the stakeholders know the impacts.

Case Study Four: Promotion system

The marketing team wants to highlight one product every week with a sale on the website. They ask the IT team to create a way for them to schedule promotions up to a year in advance, but also be able to change that schedule everyday if they desire.

First, Susan defines the problem as follows: current product display system on website only allows changes to be effective immediately. The user lacks the ability to future-date a price for a product. The user lacks the ability to create a "front page" placement for a product.

Second, Susan gathers the requirements from the marketing and billing teams on exactly how they want the new promotions system to work. The current product inventory system has a "front page" indicator and a single price. The marketing team's requirement is to be able to future-date the price and the "front page" indicator. The billing team's requirement is to receive the effective date range and the price from the inventory system in order to ensure a correct bill to the customer.

Third, Susan works with the database development team to create new database structures in the inventory system to allow the new functionality. She then meets with the GUI designers to review the database changes, and to see how they can create the functionality in the web management portal. She documents the design for both the GUI and the database in her detailed level design documents. She shares these design documents with the marketing team and billing team to ensure they sign off on them.

Fourth, she works with the PM to get the schedule completed, and then she consults with anyone who has any concerns or questions.

As we have reviewed this variety of four case studies, we see Susan go through the steps of the Systems design life cycle. Not all architects will be involved in all these steps. They will often delegate pieces of the design to different leads, or to other architects. In each of these cases, all her designs were accepted, and she had full support from her management. In real life, Susan would face a number of road blocks that would make her life difficult. When dealing with external customers or competing departments, factor in extra time for miscommunications and conflicting goals.

Survey of Software Tools

Software tools can make your architecture much easier. Let's review the ones that I've worked with.

Tool	Rating	How Often?	What it does	My Comments
Documenta tion tools				
IMB Rational Rose	*	once a few years ago	to design UML	This software gives a rigorous nature to UML design that might be useful in a team, all using the same elements.
Software Architect	**	for two years 4 years ago	to create system flows and functional system requireme nts	Gave some rigor around system names, but was slow and crashed a lot.
IMB Websphere Business Process Modeler	***	Used once or twice a year	to create system flows and functional system requireme nts, which can then run simulation s	Allows for simulations that will validate your design. This is really helpful.
VISIO	*** *	Every few months	to create any diagram	VISIO is great for creating professional looking diagrams pretty quickly. It doesn't do simulations.
PowerPoint	*** *	Daily	To create presentati ons and diagrams	PowerPoint is the quickest way to sketch out a design to share. I love the animation feature which allows me to show how the data flows thru the system.
Word	*** *	Daily	To create document ation	Word is great for documentation that won't fit on a PowerPoint slide. The table of contents allows you to create a very organized document.

Excel	*** *	Daily	To create tables of data	Excel is your go-to app for tables of data. It's good to ask yourself "Can I take this data and make it more readable in a table?"
Crimson Text Editor	*** *	Daily	To write minutes of my meetings, keep my TO-DO lists	I create a file for each project I am working on. I keep the meeting minutes in text for quick reference. The tabs in Crimson Editor allow me to keep all the current hot issues right there.
White board	*** *	Daily	To create diagrams and brainstorm with a team	Nothing beats a team brainstorming session, and the white board is central to it.
Paper	*** *	Daily	To sketch diagrams, notes, doodle	Often on a call I'll draw and write on paper. This allows me to avoids distraction by my email alerts, and I can sketch a diagram quicker on a paper, as the person on the phone is talking. This allows me to create a visualization of the subject.
napkin	*** *	Monthly	the best ideas are written on napkins	These are for when I am at a restaurant with my husband having dinner, and I suddenly think of a design that I need to capture before I forget, and I left my notepad in the car! DOH
Organization Tools				
Calendar	*** *	Daily	Keeps track of your schedule	Keep a calendar for all your work activities and one for you personal life. Some people keep them on the same calendar, but I don't. I have a Google calendar for my personal appointments, and my company calendar for work. I keep my personal

				calendar updated. When someone asks me if I can do something at a specific time, then I check and can tell them right away. Never double book. Its very stressful
File system organization method	*** *	Daily	To find your project files quickly	Here is my organization method d:\Work- Main work folder d:\Work\Administration - All administrative items like payroll, insurance, time sheets, end of year reviews d:\Work\download - any personal items that I need to store d:\Work\training - folders on each subject I've taken a class for, leadership program that I've participated in, then ran the next year, Toastmasters folder d:\Work\Projects - one file folder for each high level project. I keep one analysis.txt file for each project. Meeting-Date-Minutes.txt file for each meeting. d:\Work\Project\Project Name\- folders for each aspect or sub project

TO-DO Lists	****	Daily	To keep track of the items that must be completed.	I use a text editor like Crimson to keep track of it. I use my analysis.txt for each project to keep track of each project's to-do list and then I have one main list called TODODatecreated.txt Sometimes I use the same file for a year. My mentor taught me this method of prioritizing my TO-DO items: TO-DO Date Critical Update Billing diagram Should Do Fill data elements excel sheet Could Do Find new source for address validation During the day I go back to update my list. If something is not done yet, I note it as follows: Update Billing diagram - Waiting on Joe to give me the interface names. He said he'd get it by 2pm. As I finish each, I put the following notation at the end: Update Billing diagram - Done, sent it to the team at 4pm.
Email organization	****	Daily	To keep track of all my email	I keep all my email in my inbox without sorting it into any kind of filing system. I then move my mail in bulk to my archive directory in outlook. Search allows me to find emails I need. I create a new archive directory for each year. I keep all my mail.

Buddy Lists	****	Daily	Instant massager buddy list for easy contacts	I create a buddy group for each system and one for each project I am working on. This allows me to quickly find the contacts for each system when I need to ask them a question.
Instant messenger chats	****	Daily	Saved instant message chats allow for quick access to what the person said	I save every single chat session so that I can go back and look up the thing the person said. I go and look up things almost every day.
Communic ation Tools				
Face to face	****	Daily	Face to face is the best way to communic ate quickly	I try to meet with people face to face when I can. This allows me to develop a feel for them.
Video Conferencin g	****	Few times a year	Video conferenci ng allows you to read the body language during an important meeting that you can't physically attend	My team tries to have a team video conference every two months.
Phone	****	Daily	Next best thing to face to face	I try to call my team members regularly to keep up with them on the project and personally. I often find out about issues by talking to them.

IM	*** *	Daily	Quick means for communic ating	This is my most used communication. I can get information quickly and I can have many IM sessions going on at the same time.
Email	*** *	Daily	Formal communic ation for when you need to document the interaction .	I use email for more formal communications, documenting some event or issue, sending out meeting minutes, progress reports to my boss, sending files, contacting people not on my system. I usually send an IM or call the person after I email if its important. I hope others do the same otherwise I might never read their email.
Text	*** *	Daily	Quick means for communic ating	I use text to talk to people who are not on the company instant messenger, but I need a quick response.

Figure 17: Tools Matrix

Part 5: The Future
Future of Software Architecture

The future for software architecture is very bright and architecture will only grow and grow in its importance.

Just the beginning

The ENIAC, first digital computer, was created in 1946, and took up an entire building to house on an Army base. The commercial computer only became widely available in the late 1970's to early 1980's when Apple computer released the consumer-focused computers at affordable prices. Since then, there is a Moore's Law that shows a doubling of computing power every two years.

Thirty years later we are seeing the computer as a wearable life enhancer via smart phones. The computer enabled entire industries we couldn't have imagined in 1979, when I was born. Computers have gone from huge machines in a sealed-off room, with men wearing lab coats, to Engine management systems. People expect their computers to be easy to use, and not require any manual. This simplicity requires powerful software that can run cool on small hardware. The simpler the GUI, the better the designer is.

Businesses want more for less also. The evermore connected global market demands solutions that only software can offer. Business is interested in modeling to figure out what the market wants next. Their main question is "what does the market want?" If software can help them figure that out by crunching consumer trends data, then those systems will be in high demand.

I recently visited Cornell University, where I interviewed several students in IT-related fields. The research projects they worked on impressed me.

One used Bluetooth signals from smart phones to detect whether a person was in a room to create statistics on usage of all the rooms at the University. Once they collected all their raw data about usage, they would input that into a campus-wide environmental control system to save millions of dollars in electricity.

Another project was using radio frequency to send one byte at a time from device to device as an alternative to Bluetooth. The device could be very low-powered. The student and his team had developed a protocol similar to Ethernet, but using time division multiplexing.

This is just a few of the complex systems being developed at a university by undergraduates. As innovators understand the technology, they will think of new ways to apply it to solve problems. The problems they will be solving might not even be identified yet. This will create new opportunities for software architects who can create solutions. The more well-rounded and well-read the architect is the more they can relate and understand the opportunity and challenges at hand. When the architect is also an innovator in the business or other area, he or she will be unstoppable.

More and more complex systems

As every device becomes smart, architects will be required to create architectures to allow these devices to communicate and make decisions on how to behave. These systems will be as diverse as nanobots for medical use to deep space probes. Data architecture will become one of the main careers for which people train.

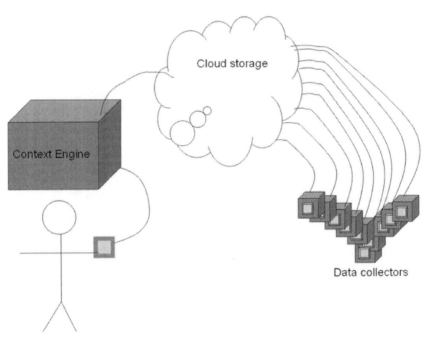

Figure 18: Data Contexting

Data contexting

Data is constantly being collected on everything: shopping trends of teenage girls in developing countries, infectious diseases spread through chickens, and self defense effectiveness. All this data is being stored in the cloud. The next objective is to create a context engine so that any user using any device can ask a question and get the answer back. The iPhone 4S is the beginning of the future. Creating context engines will be the next big thing in software architecture.

What the world needs now

The ability to analyze, design, and enhance large complex systems will be the most important IT job in the future. Right now we have the chance to create the best practices and models on which future generations of architects can build. We need leaders right now in architecture. We need bold innovators who, in each field, can create new ways of thinking about systems interaction, and can communicate that with the rest of the industry. We need societies wherein architects can communicate quickly and share information. We need a platform by which young architects can innovate and learn from mature architects. I am working on a platform called Software Architecture Symposiums International, found at http://www.sasicentral.com. This is just the beginning. Become a leader in the revolution today.

Next Steps in Your Journey

So now what? You've finished this book. In this book, you learned about what an architect is. You've learned about my path to being an architect. You've even read my five-step plan for you to become an architect. Now you need to ask yourself, "Am I ready to start my journey?" Let's look at a few things you might be going through right now as you contemplate taking your first step in the Figure Infinity system.

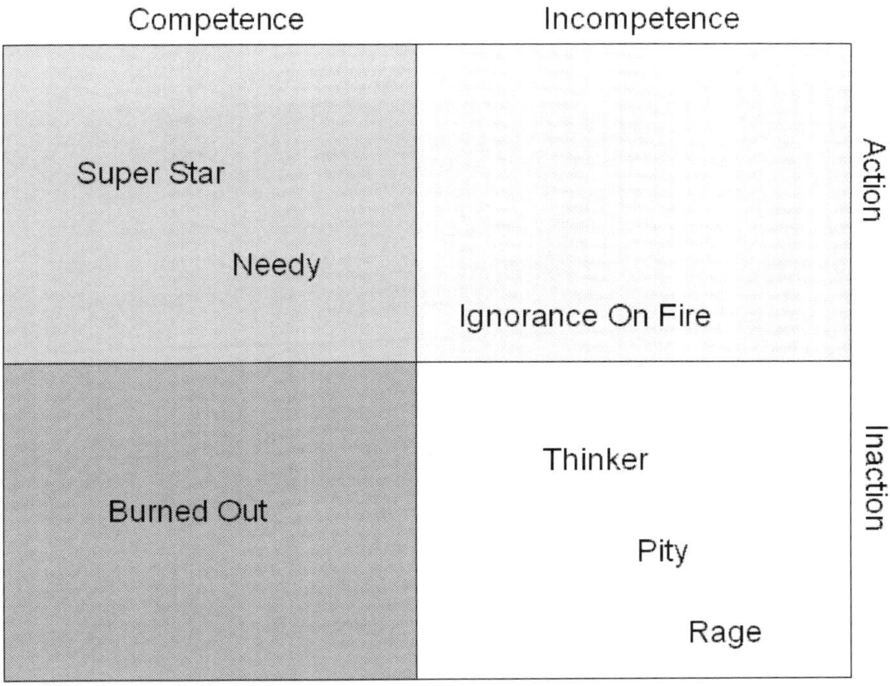

Competence	Incompetence	
Super Star Needy	Ignorance On Fire	Action
Burned Out	Thinker Pity Rage	Inaction

Figure 19: Phases of Performance

There are phases people go through when getting into a new field.

The first is the rage stage, when a person is mad at the world. They spend their time feeling victimized by their parents, teachers, friends and bosses. They might say, "If my parents had put me in a better preschool, kindergarten, elementary school, middle school, and high school, I'd have been better positioned to get into a better university and meet the right people, and then I'd be doing better today."

This feeling of victimization prevents the person from growing. The sooner a person can get out of this phase, the better. The way to get out of it is to realize that we are all dealt a hand in life. Some of us can't see, some can't walk, and some can't breathe. But no matter what, we need to do what we can with what we have. Focus on what you do have by writing a list of the things you have going for you. You'll be surprised how long the list is.

The second phase that people go through is self pity. This is when you spend time thinking about all the things you're doing wrong, and feeling hopeless about attaining your goals. They may say something like, "I screwed up again in that situation, and that's proof that I'm just a hack who will never succeed." The way to get out of the self-pity phase is to hold in your mind your goal, and the reality of where you are now at the same time, with a detailed action plan for how to achieve your goal. Ask yourself, who do I need to become to reach my goal? Then make a list of steps to get there. Then circle the first step and label it your 'Next Action.' Every day, focus on getting your next step done. Use deliberate practice and coaching to improve your performance. Ask yourself at the end of each day, "Was I better today than I was yesterday?" Prepare a Journal about the good things in your life each day.

The third phase is the thinker. This is when you spend your time just considering your next step with-out actually doing it. You read and research, and maybe even discuss and debate, but never take action. You might say, "I am not ready yet. I need to do more study. People will make fun of me. I'll be a laughing stock! I am not qualified." Self doubt fills you in this phase. The way to get out of this phase is to start small. Do something small to learn that you can do it. Once you succeed or fail, note down the things you learned. Then try again with something a little bigger or more complex. Keep trying and growing. Make sure you get feedback from your mentors. Work on one thing during each practice, and focus on it. Then afterwards review the results. Don't try to change too much at once. Focus on only one improvement at a time.

The fourth phase is the Ignorance on Fire. This is the phase where you are actually taking action. You are doing it, and you might be failing left and right, but you are really focusing on getting better. If you are in a good organization, your management should be supporting you because every time you fail, you are learning an important lesson. You are brave, and are trying new things. Make sure that you are using deliberate practice and reviewing your progress with your mentors. Again focus on one improvement at a time.

The fifth phase is needy. This is the phase where you are taking action and doing well, but you feel the need to get feedback constantly. You feel very nervous, and are filled with anxiety. You say things like, "Did I do okay? Am I failing? Will I make it?" The way to move on beyond that is to keep going, and let your mentors know to tell you if they have any feedback. Just this simple request will allow them to tell you without you begging for their insights. Let people know you are open to suggestions, but do it with confidence and the attitude that you want to improve.

The sixth phase is the superstar. In this phase you are taking action and getting it right most of the time. Make sure you that keep growing during this phase, because shifts in the world around you can cause your methods to become depreciated quickly. This is when you need to be aware of the saying, "What got you here won't get you there." Create new challenges for you to stay out of your comfort zone. Mentor, write articles, and teach. Keep fresh. Do what it takes to stay creative. You are in control of your motivation. Find out what motivated you in the past, and keep that in your life.

There is a seventh phase for which you must watch out. This phase can ruin your career. It's your responsibility to avoid this phase. This is the burnout phase. Let's look at the three things that cause burnout.

First, you can burnout quickly if you mismanage your time. Please reference the time management chapter of this book to make sure you are setting priorities and focusing on the task at hand.

Second, you can burnout quickly if you do not schedule refresh time. Refresh time is time doing things that reenergize your life force. This might be spending time with your family, exercising, being close to nature, doing sports, participating in the arts, volunteering, or any other activity that refreshes your spirit. If you haven't done one or more of these in a while, you need to schedule time to do them.

Third, you can burnout quickly if you do not live a healthy lifestyle. This means eating a balanced diet, and avoiding glucose-spiking foods like white bread, white pasta, candy, soda and processed juice. It means making sure if you do have some carbohydrates, that you need to eat some protein also. A healthy lifestyle also includes getting seven to eight hours of sleep every night. When you sleep, your brain loosens connections you haven't used and strengthens ones you use regularly, thus making your memory better. When you don't get enough sleep, your memory will fail you. As an architect, you must have a very good memory.

It's important to watch out for burnout, especially when you are doing very well. Your career is your responsibility. Manage it with care by avoiding burnout.

So, are you ready? The only way to find out is to start!

Dedication and Acknowledgements

This book is dedicated to my husband Tony Correa and my sister Julie Welzien. They supported me each morning as I wrote by making me breakfast and allowing me to focus. I started writing the book in January 2011, and finished the first draft on October 31st 2011. During this time they encouraged me many times.

Thanks to my network of mentors and supporters who've supported me during my career and my family for keeping me going. A few have been mentioned in this book, but many others have been immensely helpful also.

Thanks to my cover designer Ken Lemieux.

Thanks to my editor Chuck Van Soye.

I'd like to especially thank the folks who gave me extensive revisions and spent much time and effort including:

Georgia Welzien

Doug Woolley

Larry Hess

Greg Wicinski

Omar Alberto Moronta Tremols

Michael Ritchie

Scott Gunsaullus

Tina Chou

Thanks to my improv team including Heidi Lux, Billy Milec and Patrick McInnis who provided me with much creativity and kept my mind sharp.

Thanks to you my reader, may all your dreams of architecture be pure and as simple as possible.

Toastmasters International has given me most of the raw skills that have helped me succeed. I owe them a continuing debt which is why I am a volunteer leader in my local clubs. The meeting, communication, leadership, interpersonal communication skills I've learned came directly from practicing in my Toastmaster clubs. I highly recommend everyone attend a few meetings and see if Toastmasters could sharpen your skills. My mentors in Toastmasters have encouraged me endlessly. Thank you Toastmasters.

About the Author

Bett Correa is an enterprise architect and project manager on several premiere solutions at Verizon. She is passionate about teaching and mentoring up and coming software architects. After starting the Architects club at Verizon, she realized the need for more support for the architecture community. She speaks, writes about software architecture in the Tampa area.

Bett Correa holds a Bachelors in Computer Science from USF. She is a professional public speaker. Currently, she is the Division Governor for Toastmasters Division C of Tampa. In this role she responsible for sharpening the public speaking and leadership skills of over 700 of Tampa's Leaders.

Bett has several more books coming out soon. Keep up on the latest of her events, books, articles, speaking engagements.
Follow her on Twitter @betterworkINC.
Follow her blog at www.betterworkinc.com
Sign up for her newsletter at http://eepurl.com/f_ETX

Blog Link   Newsletter Link

Made in the USA
Charleston, SC
14 July 2013